*The Pocket Guide To*
# HOUSEPLANTS

# The Pocket Guide To
# HOUSEPLANTS

## Rob Herwig

Golden Press • New York
Western Publishing Company, Inc.
Racine, Wisconsin

Library of Congress Catalog Card Number: 82-80275
ISBN 0-307-46620-5

# CONTENTS

# COMPLETE CARE GUIDE

## CARING FOR YOUR HOUSEPLANTS

Each kind of plant has its own requirements for light, water, temperature, and the like. When you fill those particular needs, keeping your foliage plants lush and green and your flowering plants in bloom is no longer difficult. Though individual houseplants differ in their specific needs, they have much in common too. All plants need light, nutrients, water, and warmth to grow, though they differ in the necessary amounts of each. These factors work together to make a healthy plant. Lack of one cannot be compensated for by more of another. In fact, the reverse is usually true. For instance, during cool and cloudy weather, a plant's growth slows and it needs less water and nutrients.

In nature, a plant usually grows and flourishes only where the climate provides for its needs. When it is confined to a pot in your home, you are in charge of that environment. Admittedly you might not always have control over light and temperature, but you can easily control the amount of water and nutrients a plant receives with only the flick of your wrist as you wield your watering can.

Houses can provide excellent growing environments for many plants. Most tropical plants, which grow naturally in climates that are warm all year round, thrive as houseplants in homes that are heated in winter. But temperate region plants, which are designed for cold or subfreezing winters, find a heated house an alien environment.

The way to succeed with your houseplants is to try to approximate each plant's natural environment as closely as possible. You can grow a variety of plants because different parts of your home can have very different conditions. It's quite possible to grow an old-man cactus and a maidenhair fern in the same room and have the cactus behaving as if it's growing in a desert and the fern behaving as if it's growing in a forest. Place the cactus in the full sun on a southern windowsill and the fern in the bright indirect light on a table near the window. Water the fern frequently and the cactus sparingly. Mist the fern and keep it on a pebble tray filled with water. Do not mist the cactus. Pull the drapes at night around the cactus to keep it cold and let the fern enjoy the normal indoor night temperatures. Simply by treating each plant differently, you have created a mini-desert and a mini-forest in the same room.

# LIGHT

Unlike animals, plants manufacture their own food. They use the energy from light to power the chemical reaction called photosynthesis in which air and water are combined to make sugar. The sugar in turn is used to make the plant grow.

The amount of light a houseplant needs for photosynthesis is very much dependent upon its natural environment. Each kind of plant is adapted to the light conditions in its native habitat. Everyone knows that a desert-dwelling cactus and a forest-dwelling fern are accustomed to different climates. But the tricky part is, simply speaking, deciding which windowsill in your home approximates a desert and which approximates a forest!

Many plants do well near a window but out of direct sun.

The instructions in this book should take a lot of the guesswork out of caring for your plants. Plants are described as needing direct sun, bright indirect light, curtain-filtered light, or sometimes an east, west, south or north window. But the terms used need to be defined.

*Direct sun* means a location near a window that is unshaded by trees or buildings, where the sunlight shines directly on the plant's foliage. Direct sun is very bright and it casts sharp shadows. Usually plants that need direct sun do well if they receive about four hours of sun a day. An unshaded east or west window provides this.

Plants that need coolness as well as sun do better in an east window. A southern window that is unshaded all day provides more than four hours of direct sun. Plants that need a southern exposure need full sun all day long. A southern window is usually hot, especially in summer.

The majority of houseplants needs *bright indirect light*. This might mean a southern window that is shaded by a tree (but be careful that the window remains shaded as the seasons change), or a location near enough to a window to receive a lot of light reflected off walls. Bright indirect light is bright enough to cast a definite shadow.

A sheer white curtain softens the light of a southern exposure.

*Curtain-filtered light* is brighter than bright indirect light. It means a window where a sheer white curtain is used to block the direct rays of the sun. The sheer curtain softens the intensity of the sun's light and heat and can turn an otherwise too hot and sunny window into a favorable place for many plants.

*Low interior light* is a location far from a window where light is sufficient only to cast a slight shadow. This light is bright enough for you to read by comfortably, but is sufficient for only a few kinds of plants to grow and thrive.

Use a photographer's light meter to measure light intensity.

Plants don't need to have light from the sun. They can grow well with artificial light—incandescent or flourescent—providing the light is intense enough. Sometimes a position on a table beneath a lamp that is on all day may be sufficient for a plant that requires bright indirect light, and it is usually a good spot for one that grows in low light.

You can use a photographer's light meter to measure the intensity of both sunlight and artificial light. A hand-held meter or one built into a camera will do. You'll get the most accurate reading if you position a white card where you want to place your plants and measure the light reflected off the card. Set the ASA at 50 and the shutter speed at 1/125 of a second and read the $f$-stop setting. An $f$-stop of 16 to 22 is equivalent to direct sun; $f$ 8 to 11 is equal to bright indirect light and $f$ 4 to 5.6 approximates low interior light. Readings lower than these indicate there is not enough light for any houseplant to grow.

## WATER

Just as the amount of light a plant needs is determined by its natural environment, so too is the amount of water it needs. Many plants like to have *moist soil*. This means that the top of the soil should always feel damp to the touch. But moist soil should not be so wet that if you press it, puddles of water form—such soil is called *wet soil*. Only swamp or bog plants can grow in soil that is actually wet.

Some plants prefer soil that dries between waterings. When the instructions say that soil should *dry slightly between waterings*, this means that the top of the soil should be dry to the touch before the plant is watered again. You will know it's time to water when you notice that the color of the soil has changed from dark to light.

Very few plants can survive if the soil is allowed to go bone dry. But some do prefer a fair amount of dryness at the roots. These plants are described as needing the soil to *dry somewhat between waterings*. Before watering these plants, wait several days after the soil has changed from dark to light. If you stick your finger into the soil in the pot, the top inch (about two inches in large pots) will feel dry when it's time to water.

Only in the case of cactus and succulents, and then only in winter, should the soil be allowed to *dry thoroughly*. Cactus and succulents don't grow in winter: They survive on the water stored in their tissues. When they begin to deplete this stored water, the plants start to shrivel—that's when you should water. This is usually once or twice in the entire winter.

Water large plants by plunging them into the kitchen sink.

Apply water only on sunny days and then only sparingly.

The frequency of watering needed to maintain any of these levels of soil moisture is dependent upon many factors. A plant that must be kept moist may need to be watered every other day during a hot sunny week, but only once a week during cool cloudy weather. Plants in clay pots need to be watered more frequently than plants in plastic pots because water evaporates through the sides of the clay pot. During the winter, temperatures are usually cooler, light is not as strong, and plants slow down in growth—they'll need water less frequently then too.

A plant's root system fills the entire pot and when the plant is watered, the entire soil-ball should be moistened. Always add water (except in the case of cacti and succulents in winter) until it runs out the drainage hole in the bottom of the pot. Never allow the pot to stand in a saucer of water for more than half an hour—after the water has drained through the pot, empty the saucer.

Many plants that have rosettes of foliage close to the soil will rot if their crown is wet or if water gets between the foliage and remains there. Such plants are best watered from beneath. Set the pot in a saucer and fill the saucer with water. Allow the soil to soak up the water until the top of the soil becomes moist. Or you can *plunge* such plants in a sink. Fill a sink with enough water to reach about halfway up the sides of the pot and set the pot in the sink for about fifteen minutes.

If you are having difficulty telling when to water your houseplants, you can use a specially designed meter that measures soil moisture accurately. Follow the manufacturer's instructions closely.

You can use a soil moisture gauge to tell when plants need water.

Mist the air around a plant, but avoid wetting the foliage.

## HUMIDITY

Plants not only need moisture at their roots, they need moisture around their foliage. The amount of humidity plants need varies from low—desert conditions—to high—jungle conditions. However, most plants do fine at the moderate level of humidity found in houses, except in winter when the humidity is often too low. In winter, the air inside a heated house becomes drier the more it is heated. Many plants, especially those that need high humidity, suffer then.

One way to increase air humidity is by *misting*. Using an atomizer with a powerful spray, you can fill the air around a plant with moisture. You may spray the foliage of some plants directly, but the foliage on fuzzy-leaved plants often spots if it gets wet. Spray the air around such plants and in the whole room several times a day.

Set plants that need high humidity above a tray of water.

9

An air humidifier improves your plants' and your family's health.

Plants need repotting when they become root-bound.

Setting a plant above a tray of water also increases the humidity because the water evaporates into the surrounding air. Elevate the pot above the water so the soil doesn't become soggy. A *pebble tray* is an attractive way to increase the humidity. Fill a round, shallow plastic or rubber dish with large pebbles and add enough water so the water's surface is just below the level of the pebbles. Set the plants on top of the pebbles. Add water as needed. The pebble tray acts as a drainage dish too.

Probably the easiest and most effective way to increase the humidity is to install a *room humidifier*. Portable units are quite effective and you will find that one increases your family's comfort and health in the winter as well as your plants'.

## SOIL

Soil must do more than be a place for plants to anchor their roots—it must provide water, air and nutrients. The "soil" suitable for growing houseplants is most often a mixture of ingredients, one of which is actually soil. This mixture is designed so the potting medium will hold plenty of water but still remain loose and friable enough to hold air and allow roots to penetrate.

The primary ingredients of such mixes are peat moss, vermiculite and perlite. *Peat* acts like a sponge to soak up water, but it is coarse enough so it doesn't pack down. It is low in nutrients. *Vermiculite* is mica and *perlite* is volcanic rock that have been heated to very high temperatures so that they explode rather like popcorn. They improve the soil structure by adding pockets for air, but they too have very few nutrients. Vermiculite holds more moisture than perlite. A potting mix made of peat and vermiculite or perlite must have fertilizer or soil (loam) added to provide nutrients. The soil should be pasteurized to kill disease organisms.

You can buy packaged potting mixes or make them yourself. One word of caution—it is frequently difficult to tell what ingredients make up packaged potting media. Look for ones labeled "mix" and avoid using packages labeled "potting soil" since these are usually straight soil and will be too heavy for using alone. The majority of houseplants can grow in the *standard potting mix* below:

> 1 part packaged pasteurized potting soil
>
> 1 part peat moss
>
> 1 part vermiculite
>
> add 1 ounce dolomitic limestone to each 2 gallons of mix

This standard potting mix can be modified slightly

to suit finicky plants. Most ferns will appreciate *extra peat* to keep the medium constantly moist. You can add up to 2 parts peat for such plants. Plants that need a lot of nutrients benefit from *extra loam* (potting soil) or some *dried manure*.

Cactus and succulents need a soil that doesn't hold a great deal of moisture and is well-aerated. The following formula is a *standard cactus/succulent mix:*

2 parts peat moss

2 parts packaged pasteurized potting soil

2 parts builder's sand

1 part perlite

add 2 ounces dolomitic lime and 2 ounces bone meal to each 2 gallons of mix

Orchids and bromeliads need special potting media too. The epiphytic kinds, which cling to the crevices of tree branches or rocky cliffs, have roots that act primarily as anchors. The growing medium should be very well-aerated and hold moisture without ever getting soggy. A good *epiphytic orchid or bromeliad mix* is made from: osmunda fiber (the roots of a swamp fern), fir bark (bark from the white fir tree), tree fern fiber (made from the tropical tree fern's roots and bark), or sphagnum (a dried bog moss). Any of these ingredients can be used alone or mixed in different proportions. You can also buy special mixes designed for epiphytes.

Terrestrial orchids and bromeliads take up more moisture and nutrients from their roots than do epiphytes. You can also buy a medium designed for them, or make one yourself. A good *terrestrial orchid and bromeliad mix* is:

1 part packaged pasteurized potting soil

2 parts shredded fir bark

1 part perlite

add 2 ounces of bone meal for every gallon of mix

### REPOTTING

Plants should be repotted only during the growing season when their roots have filled the pot. Shift them into the next-size-larger pot. It's usually not advisable to transfer a plant into a pot that is very much larger than the previous one, since the roots won't fill the extra space and the soil won't dry out as it should.

The easiest way to remove a plant from its old pot is to cover the soil with your hand and turn the pot upside down. Rap the topside of the pot on a countertop and the mass of roots and soil should slide out.

To loosen the roots, turn the pot upside down and give it a thump.

Lay broken pieces of clay pot beneath the soil to improve drainage.

Press the soil gently around a newly potted plant.

Prepare the new pot by placing gravel or pieces of broken clay pot on the bottom and adding some potting mix. Set the root-ball into the new pot and position it so the top of the root-ball will remain at the same level as it was in the old pot. Fill in around the root-ball with more soil, pressing lightly with your fingers. Give the pot a sound thump to settle the soil, then water to wash soil into any remaining spaces.

Always use a pot with a drainage hole so you can water thoroughly and then discard excess water. Whether you choose a clay, plastic, or ceramic pot is up to your taste, though certain guidelines should be kept in mind. Clay pots evaporate water through their sides so plants will need more frequent waterings and their roots will be cooler than with plastic pots. If you tend to overwater, choose clay pots; if you tend to underwater, choose plastic or ceramic.

### FERTILIZER

Of the thirteen elements that plants must get from the soil, only nitrogen, phosphorus and potassium are used in large quantities. For the best-looking plants, you should replenish these nutrients by fertilizing the soil. Green foliage plants need plenty of nitrogen. If flowering plants are given too much nitrogen, they will grow lots of leaves but few flowers. And if cacti and succulents are overfertilized with nitrogen they will become lanky and weak and eventually rot.

Concentrated liquid fertilizer is easy to use—it can be mixed right into the watering can.

You can buy fertilizer designed for foliage plants, for flowering plants, or for cactus and succulents. The label contains three numbers, for instance 5-10-5, which tell you the percentages of the nutrients. The first number is nitrogen, the second is phosphorus, the third is potassium or potash. A fertilizer with a ratio of 1-1-1 is good for most houseplants and is considered a *high-nitrogen* fertilizer. Use a *low-nitrogen* fertilizer with a ratio of 1-5-5 for cactus, and a *high-phosphorus* fertilizer such as 6-9-5 for flowering plants.

The easiest fertilizer to use is a concentrated liquid or granular kind that you mix with water. You can usually follow the directions on the fertilizer label, but since some plants need less fertilizer than others, you may wish to dilute the fertilizer. Make *half-strength* fertilizer by measuring only half the amount of concentrate in the recommended amount of water; make *quarter-strength* fertilizer by mixing in one-fourth the amount.

Some plants, notably azaleas and gardenias, need acid soil. They suffer an iron deficiency in soil that is not acid because they can only use the form of iron found in acidic soil. Select an *acid-type* fertilizer designed for acid-loving plants for these houseplants.

## TEMPERATURE

For a plant to be successful as a houseplant, it ought to be happy growing at the temperatures people find comfortable. And for most houseplants this is not a problem. Most of the time plants do fine at whatever temperatures your home offers. But winter temperatures can pose problems. Some dormant plants need to be cold in winter, other tropical ones need to be warmer than we tend to heat our homes.

The best way to provide the proper temperature range is to experiment with different locations—some spots are warmer or colder than others. A good way to provide cactus and succulents with the required cold at night is to shut them between the drapes and a cold window pane—however, this would be death for a plant like an African violet that needs warmth.

The temperatures given in this book represent the range of temperatures at which particular plants do best. In most cases several days at a stretch with temperatures a few degrees warmer or colder will not be harmful. Plants that need *normal room temperatures* aren't particular and will grow at whatever temperatures you find comfortable. *Warm room temperatures* means not below 60°F (16°C) at night in winter. *Cool room temperatures* means a temperature between 50° and 60°F (10° and 16°C) at night in winter. Most plants prefer day temperatures 5° to 10°F (2° to 5°C) warmer than the night temperatures.

## CLIMBING PLANTS

Though many vining houseplants willingly grow with their stems cascading over the edge of a hanging container or trailing across a table, some look best and grow best if encouraged to climb. The kind of support you give them and the way you train them to grow depends upon how the vine naturally climbs.

Many tropical climbers, such as philodendron and pothos, produce aerial roots along their stems that grasp onto moist surfaces. These plants do well if you give them a sphagnum moss-covered support. Secure the vines to the bottom of the support with wire or string, and soon the roots will take hold and the vines will begin to climb. The moss should be misted so it stays moist.

Other vines climb by twisting their stems around a support. These can grow up a stout pole or be woven through a trellis. You can even tie the long stems to a wire hoop for a decorative effect.

Vines that climb by tendrils need a latticelike trellis. You can make one from wire or strings. After you initially secure the young shoots to the bottom of the trellis, the stems will climb on their own.

Some climbing plants grow best with a sphagnum moss-covered support.

Some twining vines can be trained to a wire hoop for an attractive display.

Tall leggy plants should be cut back severely in spring.

Make cuts just above a leaf.

Some stem cuttings root in plain water.

## PINCHING AND PRUNING

Many plants will grow straight and tall with nary a branch unless you take matters into your own hands. By pinching out the growing tip at the end of a stem, you break its dominance over the dormant buds at the bases of the leaves below. Once the main growing tip is removed, some of these buds will grow into branches. If you want to keep a tall-growing plant bushy and compact, you can control its growth by pinching the stem tips regularly—about once a month during the growing season.

To pinch a stem, rub the tiny leaves and soft tissue located in between the terminal leaves on a stem between your thumb and forefinger. Rub until the tissue breaks off. This "soft pinch" encourages the buds near the top of the stem to grow into branches. If you want branches to form lower down, then give a "hard pinch" by breaking off an inch or two of the stem.

Plants that have grown leggy and unsightly will need to be pruned or cut back severely. Always cut the stems back with a sharp knife or shears just above a leaf, so you won't leave behind an unsightly stub. Many plants can be cut back to within several inches of the soil. They will sprout new branches and stems from the trunk and roots. It's best to prune severely only in spring and early summer, when a plant is in active growth. New shoots and leaves will quickly appear and the plant will recover its good looks in no time at all.

## PROPAGATION

If you break off a leafy stem from a coleus and place its end in a glass of water, it will grow roots. You can then plant the rooted stem in a pot of soil and you'll have a new plant identical to the original one! Almost all plants can be propagated from stem cuttings, though many are more reluctant to root than coleus. (In this book, the term *cutting* is generally used to mean stem cuttings, though some plants can be propagated from root or leaf cuttings too.)

As a general rule, cuttings should be taken from a plant's new growth in spring or early summer. Such soft young stem tissue is the easiest to root. The cutting should be made from the terminal two or three inches of the stem and contain one or two pairs of leaves.

Though some plants will root if placed in water, it's better to stick the end of the cutting into moist sand or vermiculite. Roots formed in water have a difficult time adapting to soil once the cutting is potted up. Those formed in rooting medium adapt more readily to soil.

Because cuttings have no roots and cannot take up water, it is important to create a very humid atmosphere around them. You can do this by constructing a tent from a plastic bag—those from dry cleaners work well—and enclosing the propagation bed. Cut tiny slits in the plastic to keep the air from getting stagnant. The air should be humid enough so that a fine mist of condensation forms on the inside of the plastic. If large droplets form, make larger holes. Keep the rooting medium moist but not soggy. Cuttings should be placed in bright indirect light until roots are formed.

Some cuttings are reluctant to root. Woody stems will be encouraged to root if they are treated with *rooting hormone* powder. You can purchase rooting hormone at most garden centers—follow the directions on the label. Other plants need warmth and actually root best if the rooting medium is warmer than the surrounding air. Such plants can be given *bottom heat* by placing them in a warm spot such as the top of a refrigerator or hot water heater, or keeping them in a special propagating tray that is warmed by thermostatically controlled heating cables.

Stem cuttings root rapidly when given bottom heat supplied by heating cables.

Many plants that grow as rosettes and lack stems can be propagated from *leaf cuttings.* African violet, gloxinia, and peperomia are propagated from mature leaves with attached leafstalks. Succulents such as sedum, echeveria and jade plant can be propagated from their stalkless leaves. First roots grow from the leaves and then new leafy shoots arise. Rex begonia, snake plant and cape primrose can be propagated from pieces of their leaves. Plantlets bearing buds and roots will grow from the surface of the leaves and can be separated from the leaf piece when they are large enough. Give leaf cuttings the same warmth, light, moisture and humidity recommended for stem cuttings.

Enclose cuttings in a plastic bag to keep the humidity high.

*Cane cuttings* are pieces of woody stem from plants like corn plant, dragon tree, dumb cane and ti plant. The stems of such plants are marked with leaf scars and a dormant bud is located at each scar. Shoots will grow from these buds. Cut the stem into pieces about three inches long and then bury the pieces just beneath the surface in a container of moist potting soil. Keep the medium moist and be patient, it may be a month before any signs of growth appear.

Many tall, woody-stemmed plants can be *air-layered.* Air-layering is a slow process, but it is a sure way to propagate plants whose stem cuttings are difficult to root. To air-layer a plant, first scrape off the bark in a ring around the stem about two feet from the end of a branch. Rub rooting hormone into the wound and then wrap that area of stem with damp sphagnum

Many plants that lack stems can be propagated by leaf cuttings.

Air-layering is a good way to propagate tall plants.

Sow seeds evenly in a tray of moist propagating mix.

When seedlings have two sets of leaves, transplant them to individual containers.

moss. Cover tightly with plastic. It will be several months before you see roots peeking through the sphagnum. You can then cut off the rooted section and pot it up. Enclose the new plant in a plastic bag for several weeks.

You can often *divide* stemless plants that grow as clumps or multiple rosettes, or plants that form *offsets* (shoots growing from the base of a plant). Slide the root-ball out of the pot and gently pull the crowns apart. If the plants are attached to a common root or tuber, then cut them apart with a sharp knife, but slowly pull the tangled roots apart, disturbing as little soil as possible. Division is best done in spring or early summer.

Most houseplants are reproduced by vegetative means and not by sexual propagation (from seeds or spores). Some hobbyists however may try to grow houseplants from the seeds that form naturally on their flowering plants, or they may even try their hand at hybridizing houseplants. These hobbies are best left to the skilled plant grower, since many kinds of seeds contain germination inhibitors and need special treatments to induce them to grow.

Packaged seeds sold by nurseries have already been treated and should germinate easily. Many flowering houseplants and some tropical foliage plants can be started from purchased seed. Use a special packaged seed starting mix for best results. Moisten the medium and spread it several inches thick in a seed tray. Sprinkle very fine seed on top of the medium; larger seeds should be planted twice as deep as their diameters. A special propagator warmed with heating cables will speed things along and is especially useful for tropical foliage plants.

Cover the seed tray with plastic or glass to keep the medium moist and the humidity high, and set it in a warm location in bright indirect light. After the seedlings emerge, gradually remove the cover, but keep the medium moist. When the seedlings are large enough to handle, transplant them to another tray so they are several inches apart. When they have two sets of leaves, transplant the seedlings to individual containers or small pots to continue growing.

### INSECT AND DISEASE PESTS

Plants that are grown correctly rarely fall prey to insects or diseases, but if they do, the problem is usually easily eliminated. Underwatering or underfertilizing many plants makes them subject to insect attack. And if you overwater or keep a plant too cold, it may be easy prey for fungus disease. Good culture is the best prevention.

16

The most common insects to bother houseplants are aphids, spider mites, mealybugs and scale. Aphids are found lined-up in clusters along young succulent stems and flowers, sucking the sap from these soft tissues. You can kill the insects by swabbing the infested parts with a cotton ball soaked in rubbing alcohol. The same treatment is effective for getting rid of mealybugs, which resemble tiny cottony masses tucked into the tight places between leaves and stems.

Spider mites are so tiny they are microscopic. They infest the undersides of leaves, sucking the sap and giving the upper side of the leaves a spotted appearance. Sometimes you can notice them by the fine webs they spin. Spider mites can be eliminated by giving the plant, especially the leaf undersides, a shower. These tiny pests usually attack plants that are suffering from low humidity or underwatering. Scale insects protect themselves with hard shiny shells and are thus difficult to get rid of. You can squash each shell individually, but then swab the foliage to kill any young shell-less insects.

When these treatments fail, select a chemical insecticide designed for houseplants. For safety's sake, be sure to follow the label directions carefully. When using a spray, apply the chemical where the air is still and away from any food. Do not handle the plant until the foliage has dried. Systemic insecticides are applied to the soil in the pot and are taken up into the plant to act as a poison to any pests that might munch on the plant. These are very effective against persistent scale, but the chemicals can be absorbed through the skin, so don't handle the soil. Some plants, especially ferns, are sensitive to certain insecticides, so read the label carefully before applying the insecticide.

Diseases caused by fungus and bacteria usually strike plants that are grown under conditions that are too cool or wet, or where air is stagnant. Mildew and botrytis are troublesome leaf molds. To prevent them, keep your plants' foliage dry, and provide good air circulation by pruning plants that are too bushy. A serious disease called damping off is caused by a fungus that attacks stems of young plants, It flourishes in wet cold soil. Do not water plants on cloudy days or in the evening—if you can, wait for a sunny morning.

If you meet your houseplants' cultural needs, insect and disease problems should be few and far between. Just be sure to closely inspect newly purchased plants—you may even want to isolate them for a few weeks—so you won't inadvertently introduce pests to your collection of healthy houseplants.

Aphids suck the sap from tender new growth.

Scale insects have a hard shell and are difficult to eradicate.

Mildew can be a problem if foliage gets wet.

# HOUSEPLANTS FROM A TO Z

**ABUTILON** (Flowering Maple, Chinese-Lantern)
These colorful plants are well known for their variegated maple leaf-shaped foliage and their globe-shaped orange, salmon, red, or white flowers that bloom all year. These vigorous plants can grow from a small cutting into a thirteen-foot tree in one year but regular pinching will keep them in bounds. *Abutilon striatum* 'Thompsonii' (top) is the most popular. *Abutilon megapotamicum* has weeping stems.
**Light:** Needs at least four hours of direct sun a day for flowering. **Water:** Keep soil moist. **Temperature:** Normal room temperatures. **Soil:** Repot every month or two to keep growing vigorously. Use standard potting mix. **Fertilization:** Fertilize once a month. **Propagation:** Take cuttings from soft stems. **Special Care:** If plant becomes rangy, take cuttings and discard it.

**ACACIA armata** (Mimosa, Kangaroo Thorn)
In early spring, mimosa's arching branches are covered with pretty, yellow flowers, but those branches are also covered with thorns! Mimosa needs cool winter temperatures to set its flower buds. It grows best if kept in a cool greenhouse or a sunny enclosed porch in winter as long as the temperature is above freezing.
**Light:** Needs all-day sun. Grow outdoors in summer. **Water:** Allow soil to dry between waterings. **Temperature:** Needs low temperatures about 50°F (10°C) at night in winter to stimulate flowering. **Soil:** Repot every year or two using standard potting mix and moving into a much larger container. **Fertilization:** Fertilize once a month from spring through summer. **Propagation:** Take stem cuttings in midsummer. **Special Care:** If leaves turn brown, water more frequently.

**ACALYPHA** (Chenille Plant, Cattail, Copperleaf)
When grown under ideal conditions, the chenille plant (bottom), *A. hispida*, produces long fuzzy red or pink blossoms throughout the year. The copperleaf, *A. wilkesiana*, blooms in fall and winter, but its flowers aren't as large as the chenille plant's. The copperleaf, however, is admired for its showy foliage, which can be bronzy-green and mottled with copper, red, or purple; green with orange, red, or white markings; or russet-brown.
**Light:** Bright indirect light is best, but some direct sun is acceptable. **Water:** Keep soil moist. **Temperature:** Normal room temperatures. **Soil:** Use standard potting mix with extra peat. **Fertilization:** Fertilize monthly from spring through fall. **Propagation:** Take cuttings in midsummer. **Special Care:** Prune stems back severely in early spring.

**19**

**ACHIMENES** (Achimenes, Monkey-Faced Pansy)
These freely blooming plants are a delight from spring through fall when they produce their satiny tubular flowers. They are particularly appealing when grown at eye-level in a hanging basket. The many hybrids available offer a rainbow selection of flower colors.
**Light:** Bright indirect light. **Water:** Keep soil moist. **Temperature:** Normal room temperatures are ideal. Avoid drafts or sudden chills. **Soil:** Use one-half peat, one-quarter potting soil, and one-quarter vermiculite. **Fertilization:** Fertilize once a month with high-phosphorus fertilizer. **Propagation:** Take cuttings in spring, or divide dormant rhizomes. **Special Care:** Allow foliage to die back in fall by withholding water. Dig up rhizomes and store in cool, dry place over winter. Repot in spring; cover with one inch of soil.

**ACORUS gramineus** (Grassy-Leaved Sweet Flag)
The fine-textured leaves of this marsh plant grow in graceful fan-shaped clumps and provide a beautiful contrast to bolder-textured houseplants. *A. gramineus* 'Pusillus,' a dwarf form, grows to only three or four inches tall. Well-known varieties, which grow to a foot and a half, are 'Aureomarginatus' (middle) with yellow-striped leaves and 'Albovariegatus' with white-striped leaves.
**Light:** Green varieties can grow in low light; variegated kinds need bright indirect light. **Water:** Keep soil wet. **Temperature:** Prefers cool temperatures but tolerates warmth and drafts. **Soil:** Grow in packaged potting soil. **Fertilization:** Feed every six months. **Propagation:** Cut creeping rootstock into segments containing leaves. **Special Care:** Brown leaf tips and red spider mites may be problems in low humidity.

**ADIANTUM** (Maidenhair Fern)
These ferns with their wiry black stems and lacy foliage are among the most beautiful and the most difficult ferns to grow as houseplants. The fan maidenhair (bottom), *A. tenerum* 'Scutum Roseum,' has dense foliage that opens rosy-pink. The delta maidenhair, *A. raddianum,* is the easiest to grow, and the lovely southern maidenhair, *A. capillus-veneris,* the most demanding.
**Light:** Needs bright indirect light. **Water:** Keep very moist except in winter when soil should dry somewhat. **Temperature:** Prefers cool temperatures. **Soil:** Pot in regular potting mix with extra peat. Prefers to be slightly root-bound. **Fertilization:** Feed once in spring and once in summer with half-strength fertilizer. **Propagation:** Divide in late winter. **Special Care:** Needs high humidity or foliage will turn brown.

20

**AECHMEA** (Urn Plant, Vase Plant, Living-Vase)

Urn plants are the easiest bromeliads to grow. When in bloom they add a striking decorator's touch to almost any room with their boldly striped or variegated foliage and their dramatic flower stalks. *A. fulgens* (top) has a bright red flower stalk with blue petals. The leaves of its variety 'Discolor' are tinted violet-red on their undersides. *A. fasciata* (middle) boasts many different varieties with leaves variously striped or marbled with white. It produces a tufted pink flower stalk with blue petals. Many other species of *Aechmea* are popular.

If purchased in bloom, the urn plant can be kept in low light in the interior of a room and, if watered occasionally, will remain showy for as long as six months. The main plant slowly dies after flowering—this may take a year or more—but it produces offsets at its base, which can be propagated. If you wish to renew the plant from offsets, give the flowering urn plant the proper light and best of care.

**Light:** Bright indirect light. **Water:** Keep the vase formed by the leaves filled with water. Water the soil only after it dries out. **Temperature:** Normal room temperatures are acceptable. **Soil:** Use terrestrial orchid/bromeliad mix and use a small pot since urn plants have a shallow root system. **Fertilization:** Add one-quarter-strength fertilizer to the vase once a month. **Propagation:** Separate the offsets, being sure to include some roots, after the mother plant begins to die. **Special Care:** Mist several times a week. Clean out vase every month. Scale and mealybugs may be problems. To encourage flowering, enclose two-year-old offsets in a bag with an apple for four days.

**AEONIUM** (Saucer Plant, Pinwheel, Black Tree)

The thick flattened leaves of these succulents form rosettes that may be tucked next to each other near the soil or set atop sturdy stems. *A. arboreum* (bottom) has glossy green leaves; its variety, 'Atropurpureum,' the black tree, has dark purple foliage. The popular pinwheel, *A. haworthii*, has red-edged, blue-green leaves. **Light:** At least four hours of direct sun each day is best; bright indirect light is acceptable but foliage will be less colorful. **Water:** Allow soil to dry between waterings. Water even less during winter. **Temperature:** Normal room temperatures. Cold winter windowsills are welcomed. **Soil:** Use cactus/succulent mix. **Fertilization:** Feed with half-strength fertilizer once in spring and summer. **Propagation:** Take stem cuttings in early summer. **Special Care:** May be summered outdoors.

21

**AESCHYNANTHUS** (Lipstick Plant, Basket Plant)

The trailing stems and the whorls of tubular flowers of this gesneriad are best admired when suspended at eye-level in a hanging basket, thus the common name, basket plant. The equally curious name, lipstick plant, is descriptive of the way the tubular flowers emerge from a dark-colored "lipstick case." These plants require more light and higher temperatures than most other gesneriads.

*A. marmoratus* (top) produces golden flowers in spring to complement its speckled foliage. 'Black Pagoda' blooms throughout the year. *A. speciosus* (middle) has similar flowers but is upright growing. The scarlet flowers of *A. radicans* and *A. pulcher* appear in late winter or early spring. Many other species are cultivated.

**Light:** Provide full sun in winter; in summer, bright indirect light or morning sun. **Water:** Keep moist in summer and allow to dry somewhat between waterings in winter. **Temperature:** Normal room temperatures are acceptable, though winter temperatures should not fall below 60°F (16°C). **Soil:** Use standard gesneriad mix. **Fertilization:** Fertilize monthly from spring through fall. **Propagation:** Take stem cuttings in spring or early summer after flowering. Place several rooted cuttings in a pot in order to produce a full-looking plant. **Special Care:** Cut back stems to about six inches after blooming to encourage new growth. Provide high humidity and keep away from drafts. Do not move while flower buds are forming and during bloom to prevent blossoms from dropping.

**AGAPANTHUS** (African Lily, Lily-of-the-Nile)

Large clusters of lilylike flowers appear all summer long if you give African lily a place in the sun. *A. africanus* grows two to three feet tall and produces thirty or more lavender-blue flowers to a cluster. *A. orientalis* is taller-growing and produces up to a hundred blooms in a cluster. Flowers come in light blue, dark blue, or white. Dwarf and variegated varieties are available too.

**Light:** Needs direct sun all day. **Water:** Keep moist during growing season; dry while dormant. **Temperature:** Room temperatures during growth; 40° to 45°F (4° to 7°C) at night during winter. **Soil:** Use standard potting mix. **Fertilization:** Feed monthly during growth. **Propagation:** Divide rhizomes every few years in spring. **Special Care:** Allow leaves to die and plant to go dormant by withholding water in fall. Blooms best when roots are crowded.

22

## AGAVE (Agave, Century Plant)

These mighty succulents grow in large rosettes of stiff swordlike leaves whose edges and tips are frequently armed with stout thorns. The name century plant originated because the plants are reported to live for a hundred years before sending up flowering stalks. They die after seeds are set. Actually, century plants flower and die anywhere between ten and fifty years of age and the offsets that grow at their bases live on after the main plants die.

*A. americana* (top) is a very popular species. Its leaves may be solid blue-green, but are frequently bright green and edged or striped with bold yellow. This is a very large plant and it is hard to confine even when grown indoors in a tub. A smaller-growing agave is *A. ferox* (middle) with steel-blue leaves adorned with dark spines.

The Queen Victoria agave, *A. victoriae-reginae*, is a very pretty houseplant. It remains compact and its foliage is quite sleek, having very narrow white stripes along the margins and a single spine at the tips. Another good agave for a houseplant is *A. filifera*. Its dark green leaves are bordered with fine threadlike hairs instead of thorns.

**Light:** At least four hours of direct sun each day. **Water:** Allow soil to dry somewhat between waterings during the growing season; water only enough to keep plant from shriveling in winter. **Temperature:** Normal room temperatures are fine, though cold winter nights are desirable. **Soil:** Use standard cactus/succulent mix. **Fertilization:** Apply bone meal each spring. **Propagation:** Divide in spring or summer. **Special Care:** Needs low humidity. Repot only every few years.

## AGLAONEMA (Chinese Evergreen, Aglaonema)

These low-growing, bushy foliage plants are valued because they produce their showy leaves under low light conditions. 'Silver King' (bottom) with dark green and silver leaves, 'Snow Queen' with leaves and stems marbled creamy-white, and 'Francher' with narrow green leaves banded with silver are popular varieties.

**Light:** A northern window or bright interior light. **Water:** Keep soil moist during growing season; allow to dry between waterings in winter. **Temperature:** Prefers warm temperatures. Keep away from drafts. **Soil:** Use standard potting mix. **Fertilization:** Feed every three months. **Propagation:** Divide basal shoots or air-layer. **Special Care:** Leaves curl and turn brown if temperature is too cold or humidity is too low.

## ALLAMANDA (Allamanda, Golden-Trumpet)

Allamanda produces its large trumpet-shaped flowers all summer long and its vining stems can grow to great lengths over the growing season. 'Grandiflora' is a dwarf form whose compact growth makes it a suitable houseplant; other varieties do best when grown in a greenhouse.

**Light:** Provide at least four hours of direct sun each day. **Water:** Keep soil moist and water frequently during growth; allow to dry some during winter. **Temperature:** Normal room temperatures. **Soil:** Use standard potting mix with some extra peat. **Fertilization:** Apply every two weeks during growing season. **Propagation:** Take cuttings from new growth in spring. **Special Care:** Needs high humidity. Provide support for climbing stems. Cut stems back to six inches in fall; water less and move to a cool spot until spring.

## ALOCASIA (Elephant's-Ear Plant)

Giant glossy heart-shaped leaves with prominent veins characterize the elephant's-ear plant. These dramatic-looking plants require warm temperatures and high humidity and are more difficult to grow in the home than in a greenhouse.

**Light:** Needs very bright indirect light from a southern or eastern exposure. **Water:** Keep moist during the growing season; allow to dry somewhat in winter. **Temperature:** Warm temperatures during growing season; keep cool, 60° to 65°F (16° to 18°C), during dormant period. **Soil:** Grow in pure sphagnum moss. **Fertilization:** Apply monthly during growing season. **Propagation:** Divide rootstock. **Special Care:** Needs high humidity. Give winter rest by withholding water and providing cool temperatures for several months.

## ALOE (Aloe, First-Aid Plant, Candelabra Plant, Crocodile-Jaws)

The long curved leaves of an aloe plant are arranged in a tight rosette and are often spotted or warted with white. Tiny sharp or soft teeth line the edges. The most famous of these succulents is the first-aid plant, *A. barbadensis*, whose leaves ooze a sticky sap, when broken, that is used for healing burns. Another small-growing species for indoor culture is crocodile-jaws, *A. humilis*. Its blue-green leaves have white teeth on their edges and white spots on the undersides. *A. variegata* (opposite, top) grows to nine inches tall and is colored blue-green with coppery tones appearing in strong light.

The candelabra plant (opposite, bottom), *A. arborescens*, grows into a small tree indoors, with a rosette of blue-green leaves topping the woody stem. If given enough light, this aloe will send up a stalk of scarlet flowers.

**Light:** Grow in sunny south, east, or west window. **Water:** Allow soil to dry between waterings during the growing season; during winter, water only enough to keep the leaves from shriveling. **Temperature:** Normal room temperatures are acceptable, though cool nights in winter are beneficial. A winter windowsill is excellent. **Soil:** Use standard cactus/succulent mix. **Fertilization:** Fertilize once in spring and once in summer with low-nitrogen fertilizer. **Propagation:** Divide offsets from parent plant; allow cut surface to dry for several days before putting in propagation medium. **Special Care:** Prefers low humidity. Will rot if overwatered.

## AMPELOPSIS brevipedunculata 'Elegans' (Colored Grape-Leaf)

The thin, vining red stems of this graceful foliage plant can be allowed to trail from a hanging basket or be trained to climb up a support. The leaves are variously shaped, having no lobes or up to five lobes, and are attractively streaked with pink and white.

**Light:** Provide bright indirect light. **Water:** Allow to dry somewhat between waterings. **Temperature:** Needs night temperatures of about 40°F (4°C) in the winter; a north windowsill may be sufficiently cold. **Soil:** Use standard potting mix. **Fertilization:** Fertilize once a month during the growing season. **Propagation:** Take cuttings in summer. **Special Care:** Pinch or cut back as needed to keep plant in bounds.

## ANANAS (Pineapple)

Several species of pineapple, a member of the bromeliad family, make excellent houseplants, though the edible pineapples they produce are less tasty than they are ornamental. *A. comosus* 'Variegatus' (bottom) is a stunning plant with yellow-striped leaves. *A. nanus* grows to only fifteen inches tall.

**Light:** Needs direct sun all day. **Water:** Allow soil to dry between waterings. Keep cup formed by leaves full of water. **Temperature:** Normal room temperatures are acceptable. **Soil:** Use standard orchid/bromeliad mix. **Fertilization:** Apply half-strength fertilizer once a month. **Propagation:** Cut off leafy top from fruit; allow to dry for several days and root in vermiculite. **Special Care:** Provide high humidity by misting or by using pebble tray.

## ANTHURIUM (Flamingo Flower, Flamingo Lily, Tailflower)

If you can provide enough humidity and warmth, these tropical beauties will produce their unusual blooms throughout the year. The flamingo flower (top), *A. scherzeranum*, grows to only a foot tall and its flower, a heart-shaped spathe with a curling spadex in the center, blooms in red, pink, or white. This small plant is the easiest to grow of all the anthuriums since it is the most tolerant of dry air.

Tailflower (middle), *A. andraeanum*, grows about two-feet tall and produces large flowers that are often grown as cut flowers for florists. The showy bracts come in a variety of colors, ranging from a black-red to salmon-pink. It demands a higher humidity and is a more temperamental plant than the flamingo flower. **Light:** Bright indirect light is needed for flowering. **Water:** Keep soil constantly moist but not soggy during the growing season. Allow to dry slightly during winter. **Temperature:** Needs warm temperatures. May be harmed at temperatures below 60°F (16°C). **Soil:** Use one-part sphagnum moss and one-part fir bark. **Fertilization:** Apply quarter-strength fertilizer every two weeks. **Propagation:** Remove root-bearing side-shoots. **Special Care:** Cover any roots that grow on soil surface with moist sphagnum moss. Keep humidity high by misting or by using a pebble tray. Brown or yellow leaf tips and edges indicate too low a humidity or too high a temperature.

## APHELANDRA (Zebra Plant, Saffron-Spike)

Zebra plants are outstandingly colorful houseplants. Their dark glossy foliage is decorated with prominent white veins, making them ornamental throughout the year. For a month or two in fall, they are even more showy when flower stalks festoon every stem tip. *A. squarrosa* is a compact plant with golden-yellow flowers. *A. aurantiaca* grows larger and has orange-red blooms.

**Light:** Needs bright indirect light. **Water:** Keep moist except during the winter when soil should dry somewhat. **Temperature:** Normal room temperatures. **Soil:** Use standard potting mix with some extra peat added. **Fertilization:** Feed every two weeks with half-strength fertilizer. **Propagation:** Take stem cuttings in spring; use rooting hormone. **Special Care:** Cut back severely in spring or plant will become leggy. Leaves drop readily if soil dries out. Needs high humidity.

**APOROCACTUS flagelliformis** (Rattail Cactus)
This cactus has long trailing stems that can grow to as
long as three feet. Suspend the plant in a hanging
basket in a sunny window where its red bristles will
catch the light and the stems will have plenty of room.
If given enough sun, the rattail cactus produces beautiful crimson-pink blossoms in spring.
**Light:** At least four hours of direct sun a day to encourage bloom; grows well but may not bloom in
bright indirect light. **Water:** Allow soil to dry somewhat during growing season; water once a month
during winter. **Temperature:** Room temperatures during the growing season; colder temperatures during
winter. **Soil:** Use cactus/succulent mix. **Fertilization:**
Feed once in spring. **Propagation:** Take cuttings; allow
to dry several days before putting in rooting medium.
**Special Care:** Will rot if overwatered.

**ARAUCARIA heterophylla** (Norfolk Island Pine)
The tiered branches and symmetrical growth of the
Norfolk Island pine make it a particularly handsome
houseplant. It grows slowly, putting out one new tier
of branches a year, but eventually it can reach six or
more feet tall.
**Light:** Bright indirect light. **Water:** Keep moist during
the growing season; allow to dry slightly during the
winter. **Temperature:** Normal room temperatures during the growing season; cool temperatures are prefer-
able in winter. **Soil:** Use standard potting mix. **Fertilization:** Apply monthly during the growing season.
**Propagation:** By seed. **Special Care:** Needs high humidity in winter. Leaf browning and drop is due to
low humidity or soil dryness. Lower branches die with
age, but will drop prematurely if humidity and soil
moisture are inadequate.

**ARDISIA crenata** (Coralberry)
Coralberry's green berries ripen to a gleaming red in
fall and may still be clinging to the branches in spring
when fragrant pink or white flowers appear. This attractive plant looses its lower branches with time and
grows into a three-foot-tall tree, but the branches can
be cut back in spring for a more bushy shape.
**Light:** Bright indirect light. **Water:** Keep soil moist.
**Temperature:** Normal room temperatures during the
growing season; cool nights during winter. **Soil:** Standard potting mix. **Fertilization:** Feed every two weeks
with half-strength fertilizer. **Propagation:** Take cuttings in spring. **Special Care:** Main stems may be cut
back to two inches in spring; keep soil dry until new
growth sprouts. Hand pollinate flowers with a paint
brush to encourage abundant berries.

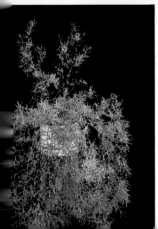

**ASPARAGUS** (Asparagus Fern, Sprengeri, Lace Fern)
There are several very popular species and varieties of asparagus fern. All of them are noted for their billowy green branches and ease of culture. Not ferns at all, but relatives of edible asparagus, asparagus ferns have shoots that, as they emerge from the soil, resemble asparagus spears.

Another unfernlike characteristic of these plants is that they thrive in dry air. They grow with abandon even when suspended above radiators and hot air vents. As long as their soil is kept moist, low atmospheric humidity seems to cause no ill effects. Also they can adjust to many different light conditions, ranging from low light to direct sun.

The most popular asparagus fern is *A. densiflorus* 'Sprengeri' (bottom). Its airy fine-textured stems are best displayed when allowed to cascade from a hanging basket. Keep it out of the way, however, since there are tiny thorns scattered along the stems. Tiny white flowers followed by red berries appear in summer on plants receiving good light. 'Myersii' (top) displays more compact, upright stems. 'Myriocladus' (middle) is a bushy plant.

Another commonly grown species is *A. setaceus* (sometimes called *A. plumosus*), the lace fern. Its long lacy branches have very tiny needles and are often used by florists in flower arrangements. It has a vining habit and is best displayed in a large window where it can ramble at will. *A. retrofactus* is similar in appearance, but has long bright green needles and tends to climb in a zigzag pattern.

**Light:** Does best in bright indirect light, but will tolerate a half day of full sun or low light. **Water:** Keep soil moist but not soggy. **Temperature:** Normal home conditions are fine. Can tolerate winter night temperatures down to 50°F (10°C). Avoid prolonged extreme heat. **Soil:** Use standard potting mix. Repot annually or as soon as the vigorous root system fills the pot. **Fertilization:** Apply monthly during the growing season. **Propagation:** Divide in spring. **Special Care:** Yellow, brown-edged foliage and leaf drop are due to lack of soil moisture or to too much light. Yellow foliage without brown edges is due to low light. Plants form large fleshy roots that can completely fill a pot and even break it if the plant is allowed to remain potbound. Repot annually into a larger pot. Overwatering will quickly lead to root rot.

28

**ASPIDISTRA elatior** (Cast-Iron Plant, Barroom Plant)
Because this undemanding plant survives with the most minimal care, it is often called the cast-iron plant. However, with a small amount of attention it can grow into a handsome three-foot-tall specimen. It is oblivious to low humidity and the green-leaved variety grows quite well in dim interior light. The variegated variety (top), on the other hand, needs more light or its yellow stripes will be dull.
**Light:** Tolerates dim light; does best in a north window. Full sun is harmful. **Water:** Allow to dry somewhat between waterings. **Temperature:** Tolerant of a wide range of temperatures. **Soil:** Use standard potting mix. **Fertilization:** Feed once a month during the growing season. **Propagation:** Divide in spring. **Special Care:** Will rot if overwatered.

**ASPLENIUM nidus** (Bird's-Nest Fern)
The dark-veined fronds of the bird's-nest fern are most unfernlike because they are smooth and undivided. These leathery bright green leaves can grow as long as three feet, though most bird's-nest ferns remain more compact if grown indoors.
**Light:** A north window or bright indirect light. **Water:** Keep moist during the growing season, but allow to dry somewhat during winter. **Temperature:** Normal room temperatures are acceptable. Cool nights are best during the winter. **Soil:** Use half potting soil and half peat moss. **Fertilization:** Feed once in spring and once in summer with half-strength fertilizer. **Propagation:** Can be increased from the spores that form on the leaf undersides. **Special Care:** Place on pebble tray and mist frequently to provide high humidity. Cut off yellow leaves at their bases.

**ASTROPHYTUM myriostigma** (Bishop's Cap)
This unusual cactus resembles a wooly softball more than a cactus. Its five broad ribs are spineless and its smooth gray-green surface is covered with fine white hairs. More likely to bloom when grown as a houseplant than most cacti, the bishop's cap produces yellow flowers in summer.
**Light:** Four hours of direct sun a day. Also does well in bright indirect light. **Water:** Allow soil to dry somewhat between waterings from spring through fall. Water once a month in winter. **Temperature:** Normal room temperatures during the growing season. Cold nights, such as those on a windowsill, are needed in winter. **Soil:** Standard cactus/succulent mix. **Fertilization:** Apply bone meal in spring. **Propagation:** Use seeds from fruits that follow the blossoms. **Special Care:** Avoid intense summer sun.

29

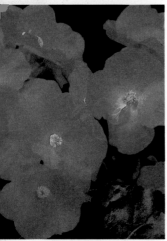

## BEGONIA (Begonia)

Some begonias are grown purely for their ornamental foliage and others for their magnificent flowers, but many kinds offer both beautifully colored foliage and delightful flowers. The begonias are such a diverse group of plants that no collection of houseplants is complete without several specimens. Indeed, some people collect only begonias and there are enough varieties to fill a greenhouse without any duplication.

There are three basic types of begonias, classified according to their root systems. The fibrous-rooted begonias have shallow systems of fine roots. The rhizomatous-rooted kinds grow from thick, hairy rootstocks that creep along near the surface of the soil and store water. Tuberous-rooted begonias have fat storage tubers where food and water are stored, and have a dormancy period each year during which the tops of the plants die back to the roots. There are both foliage and flowering begonias among the fibrous and the rhizomatous begonias. The tuberous begonias are grown for their large showy flowers.

In general, fibrous-rooted kinds require more water than the rhizomatous-rooted or the tuberous-rooted kinds. All begonias require well-aerated, water-retentive soil high in organic matter.

The rhizomatous rex begonias are famous for their fabulous foliage. Shaped like large lopsided hearts, the leaves are marked with an overlay of colors—pink, red, maroon, silver, rust, or lavender—with green appearing only occasionally as a bordering band. The undersides of the leaves and their stalks are frequently a rich burgundy color. They grow from rhizomes that creep along near the surface of the soil. Favorite varieties of rex begonia (there are hundreds of named varieties) are: 'Merry Christmas' with red, silver and green leaves; 'Silver Queen' with a heavy silvery sheen overlaying a green background; and 'Yuletide' with red, gold and rust foliage.

Rex begonias are the most temperamental houseplants of the group, partly because they demand a high humidity. They are easy to keep in a greenhouse, but with lots of love and attention can thrive in a house. They have the intriguing ability to sprout new plants from the veins of leaf cuttings.

Other well-known foliage-type rhizomatous begonias are less demanding than the rex types. *B. masoniana*, the iron-cross begonia, has an oddly puckered, light green leaf covered with short stiff red hairs and marked with a distinctive chocolate-brown crosslike

Pictured on this page: *Begonia corallina* (top), *B. reiger-elatior* (middle) and *B. erythrophylla* (bottom).

pattern in the center. *B. heracleifolia* is grown for its pointed-lobed bronzy-green leaves that may be marked with pink, red, or black spots. The eyelash begonia, *B. boweri*, is a small plant and boasts long pointed leaves with finely-haired margins and irregular brown blotches along the edges.

The begonias grown for their flowers can be divided into three groups: the cane begonias, which form tall bamboolike stalks and without pruning can grow to six feet tall; the bush-types, which remain small; and the trailing-types, which are best displayed from hanging baskets.

The most popular flowering begonia is the fibrous-rooted wax begonia, *B. semperflorens*. It blooms non-stop, producing masses of small pink, white, or red flowers. Its rounded foliage may be green, bronze, or variegated with white. The wax begonia is also very easy to grow.

*B. corallina*, the angel-wing begonia, is a cane begonia with many beautiful varieties. The leaves, which are slender and pointed, are frequently adorned with silver spots and have red undersides. The fragrant flowers are pink, white, or red. *B. maculata* blooms in summer, bearing pendulous pink or white flower clusters. It remains fairly compact and the glossy foliage is spotted with silver.

The beefsteak begonia, *B. erythrophylla*, has large round green leaves and bright red undersides. The light pink flowers are borne on long stems in winter and spring.

The reiger-elatior hybrid begonias have become a favorite holiday gift plant. Their enormous blossom clusters come in a vibrant array of colors: red, pink, salmon, yellow, orange and white. And their glossy pointed-lobed foliage is attractive even when the plants are out of bloom.

*B. metallica*, the metallic-leaf begonia, is a rhizomatous-type grown for its olive-green leaves veined with purple. Flowers appear throughout the summer in huge bluish-white or light rose clusters.

Famous for their flowers, the tuberous begonia, *B. tuberhybrida*, grows from a tuber, which should be allowed to go dormant during the winter. The flowers come in every color and shape imaginable. They may mimic camellias, roses, or daffodils, or be frilled or crested. Individual flowers may measure up to six inches across and are borne in clusters of two or three blooms.

**Light:** Bright indirect light is best. A northern expo-

Pictured on this page: *Begonia heracleifolia* (top), *B. maculata* (middle) and *B. masoniana* (bottom).

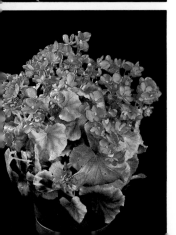

sure is also good. Direct sunlight must be avoided, except for a few hours during the winter when it may be beneficial. **Water:** Begonias are very temperamental about how they are watered. The soil must be moist during the growing season but should not be soggy. Overwatering will quickly lead to rot, but underwatering will cause leaf scorch and affect a plant's vigor. **Temperature:** Normal room temperatures are fine, but extreme heat coupled with dry air is detrimental. Cool temperatures, down to 55°F (13°C) at night, are recommended in winter. Avoid cold or hot drafts. **Soil:** The key to growing begonias successfully is in the soil. A well-draining but water-retentive soil is essential. A mixture of one-part potting soil and two-parts peat moss is ideal. Grow begonias in pots that are wider than tall, because they have a shallow root system and may rot if grown in deep pots. **Fertilization:** Feed weekly during the growing season with quarter-strength fertilizer. Do not fertilize during the winter months. **Propagation:** All begonias can be propagated from stem cuttings taken in spring or summer. The rex begonias can be propagated from leaf cuttings. Remove a large leaf and make cuts in the veins on the underside of the leaf. Place it on moist sand or vermiculite and pin the leaf to the soil surface with hairpins or toothpicks. New plants will sprout from the cut area. When these are rooted, separate them from the leaf. Begonias with rhizomes or tubers may be divided in spring. Be sure each division has leaves and roots. **Special Care:** Begonias need high humidity. Place them on pebble trays for best results. Do not mist the foliage or flowers directly since they are very susceptible to fungus and bacterial diseases, which flourish on wet foliage. Mildew shows up as powdery white patches on the leaves. Bacterial leaf spot shows up as brown blistered spots. Botrytis (gray mold fungus), grows on fallen flowers and foliage. Keep plants tidy and remove all faded leaves and flowers. Destroy infected plant parts.

Pictured on this page: *Begonia metallica* (top), *B. rex* (middle) and *B. semperflorens* (bottom).

### BELOPERONE guttata (Shrimp Plant)

The shrimp plant's flower clusters, made up of salmon-pink overlapping bracts, droop and curl in such a way that they truly resemble shrimps. The white petals that peek from beneath the bracts are not long-lasting, but the bracts themselves remain showy for months. The shrimp plant also appears under the name *Justicia brandegeana*.

**Light:** At least four hours of direct sun a day. **Water:** Keep moist during the growing season; allow to dry somewhat in winter. **Temperature:** Normal room temperatures; cool nights in winter. **Soil:** Standard potting mix. **Fertilization:** Feed every two weeks with half-strength fertilizer. **Propagation:** Take cuttings in spring. **Special Care:** Cut back plant halfway in spring to encourage new growth.

### BILLBERGIA nutans (Queen's-Tears)

This billbergia is the easiest of the bromeliads to grow and bloom. Its graceful grassy leaves are arranged in loose rosettes that form freely at the base of older ones. Eventually the pot will be full of rosettes and several will flower at the same time, producing rose-hued stems topped with weeping flower clusters. Many hybrids are available.

**Light:** Bright indirect light in summer; four hours of direct sun in winter. **Water:** Let soil dry between waterings. Keep cup formed by leaves filled with water. **Temperature:** Normal room temperatures. **Soil:** Bromeliad mix. **Fertilization:** Apply quarter-strength fertilizer to moist soil once a month. **Propagation:** Divide in spring. **Special Care:** Mist occasionally; needs less humidity than most bromeliads.

### BLECHNUM (Hammock Fern, Deer Fern)

The hammock fern (bottom), *B. occidentale,* and the deer fern, *B. spicant,* are among the easiest of the ferns to grow as houseplants. Their strong upright fronds have leathery leaves that withstand dry indoor air. The hammock fern creeps along the soil surface, sending up new clumps of fronds that change from a pink coil into a coppery-colored leaf before maturing to dark green. The deer fern is similar in appearance, but its fronds grow larger—up to two feet long.

**Light:** Bright indirect light for the hammock fern; north light for the deer fern. **Water:** Keep soil moist. **Temperature:** Normal room temperatures. **Soil:** Standard potting mix with some extra peat. **Fertilization:** Apply monthly during the growing season. **Propagation:** Divide in spring. **Special Care:** Trim off dead older fronds.

**BOUGAINVILLEA** (Bougainvillea, Paper Flower)
Whether pruned into a bush form or allowed to climb up a trellis, bougainvillea will astound you with its masses of papery flowers. Red, magenta, violet, pink, orange, or white bracts surround tiny white petals. The petals themselves don't last long, but the bracts remain colorful for months. New plants bloom freely from spring through summer, but are difficult to re-bloom unless they get a dormant period and full sun.
**Light:** Full sun all day. **Water:** Keep soil moist except in winter. **Temperature:** Room temperatures in summer; cooler in winter. **Soil:** Standard potting mix. **Fertilization:** Feed every other week during growth. **Propagation:** Take stem cuttings in spring. **Special Care:** Needs high humidity. In fall, withhold water and food, and keep in a cool place to go dormant.

**BROWALLIA** (Browallia, Sapphire Flower)
Browallia is a delightful flowering plant for winter bloom. It blossoms for months on end, producing star-like flowers colored dark blue, blue-violet, or white. The upright stems are somewhat weak and floppy, and form a gentle mound that's perfect in a hanging basket. An annual that by its nature dies after flowering, browallia is best discarded after blooming ceases. It may be renewed however from cuttings.
**Light:** Bright indirect light in summer; direct sun in winter. Avoid burning hot sun coupled with dry air. **Water:** Keep soil moist. **Temperature:** Normal room temperatures. **Soil:** Standard potting mix. **Fertilization:** Feed every other week. **Propagation:** Take cuttings anytime. **Special Care:** Leaf-drop is due to too much hot sun and lack of water. Pinch to encourage branching. Whitefly can be a problem.

**BRUNFELSIA australis** (Yesterday-Today-and-Tomorrow)
The extraordinary flowers of this plant open purple, fade to lavender the next day, and bleach to white on the third day. This chameleon action results in blossoms of three different colors on one plant! If you meet its somewhat demanding cultural needs, your yesterday-today-and-tomorrow will blossom tomorrow, tomorrow and tomorrow.
**Light:** Very bright light but out of direct sun. **Water:** Keep soil moist during growth; allow to dry during dormancy. **Temperature:** Normal room temperatures; cool during dormancy. **Soil:** Standard potting mix with extra peat. **Fertilization:** Feed every two weeks during growth. **Propagation:** Take stem cuttings in spring. **Special Care:** Must have a dormant period in late fall and again in spring.

34

**CALADIUM** (Caladium, Mother-In-Law Plant)

The large heart-shaped leaves of the caladium are papery, translucent and beautifully variegated. Pink, red, salmon, silver and white can mark the veins, which contrast with a green background, or the reverse combination of green veins and colored background is possible. Some kinds of caladium offer a combination of colors and may have ruffled or undulating leaf margins. Many varieties and hybrids are available. 'Candidum' (middle) is one of the most popular, bearing white leaves with green veins. 'Pink Beauty' (top) is a soft pink with rose ribs and a green border. 'Mrs. Arno Nehrling' is snow-white with a network of contrasting blood-red veins. 'Blaze' is almost solid red.

**Light:** Bright indirect light or light from a north window. **Water:** Keep moist during the growing season; withhold water during dormancy. **Temperature:** Must have warm temperatures. Do not place where temperature falls below 60°F (16°C) at night. Keep away from cold drafts. **Soil:** Use standard potting mix. **Fertilization:** Feed monthly during growth, beginning when leaves first appear. **Propagation:** Small tubers can be split off from large dormant tubers. Allow cut surface to dry for several hours before potting. **Special Care:** Start tubers in March. Plant about two inches deep, water, and place in a warm, humid location. After leaves are well developed, less warmth and humidity are acceptable. In fall, withhold water and fertilizer and allow leaves to die back. Store at 60°F (16°C) until spring. Alternately, start tubers in fall and give summer dormancy. Increase humidity with a pebbletray or by misting.

**CALANTHE** (Calanthe)

In fall, *C. vestita* drops its leaves and goes into dormancy, but in midwinter a flower stalk emerges from the dead-looking pseudobulb, putting on a show of white flowers whose lips may be tinted pink, orange, or red. Other species of this orchid, though they go into winter dormancy, are evergreen and bloom in spring or summer.

**Light:** Bright indirect light or curtain-filtered light in summer. Direct sun for four hours each day in winter. **Water:** Keep evergreen species moist; allow deciduous species to dry out in winter. **Temperature:** Needs warm days with a 10°F (5°C) drop at night. **Soil:** Grow in a terrestrial orchid mix. **Fertilization:** Feed twice a month during growth. **Propagation:** Divide pseudobulbs once new growth begins. **Special Care:** Keep dry and cool during dormancy.

35

**CALATHEA** (Calathea, Peacock Plant, Rattlesnake Plant, Zebra Plant)

If you have the patience to cater to their demands, the calatheas will reward you with their rich-colored foliage and uncommon good looks. These ornamental plants with beautifully banded or spotted leaves are similar in appearance to the marantas, or prayer plants, but they are even more difficult to grow because they are so demanding about light, water and humidity conditions.

Most species are cultivated for their foliage alone, but *C. crocota* (top) is grown for its deep-hued foliage and its yellow flower stalks. The rattlesnake plant (middle), *C. lancifolia* and *C. insignis,* has long stiff, boldly striped leaves with deep maroon undersides. Often confused with the prayer plant, the peacock plant (bottom), *C. makoyana,* is the most commonly grown species and adapts best to house conditions. Its creamy and olive-green blotched leaves are maroon on the undersides and the young leaves often emerge tinted maroon. The zebra plant, *C. zebrina,* has long velvety yellow-green leaves with bands of yellow along the veins. Another favorite is *C. ornata,* whose rich green leaves are marked with pink or white lines along the veins.

These plants are easy to grow in a greenhouse, but can be cultivated indoors if steps are taken to keep the humidity high. Grow them in a terrarium, on a pebble tray, or in a humidified room. Arranging them among a group of plants may raise the humidity enough around the foliage to keep the plant healthy.

**Light:** Bright indirect light is essential for keeping the foliage colorful. Direct sun will bleach and burn the foliage; low light will make the foliage too green. **Water:** Keep the soil moist but not soggy and never let the root ball dry out. Reduce watering in winter. **Temperature:** Normal room temperatures but avoid extreme heat, and warm and cold drafts. Keep where night temperatures in winter will not fall below 60°F (16°C). **Soil:** Use standard potting mix with some extra peat added. Repot every spring into fresh soil and place in pot that is wider than deep. **Fertilization:** Apply every two weeks using half-strength fertilizer. Sensitive to fertilizer salt build-up. **Propagation:** Plants may be divided in spring when repotting. Stem cuttings may also be taken but need warmth to root. **Special Care:** Keep humidity high; leaf edges turn brown and leaves drop if it is too low. Yellow lower leaves are due to underwatering. Limp, rotting stems are due to overwatering or to cold temperatures. Plants have a dormant period in winter when they should not be fed and watering should be reduced.

36

**CALCEOLARIA** (Pocketbook Plant, Slipperwort)

The curious-looking flowers of this florist plant are inflated pouches colored yellow, orange, red, or white and speckled with a darker color. Usually purchased in bloom in the spring, if kept cool and in a brightly lit spot, the pocketbook plant will be a colorful attraction for a month or so. After the flowers fade, the plant is best discarded, for it will not bloom again.

**Light:** Bright indirect light. **Water:** Keep soil moist but not soggy. **Temperature:** Flowers will last longest if temperatures are kept cool. **Soil:** No need to repot. **Fertilization:** Not necessary. **Propagation:** Nurserymen propagate pocketbook plants by sowing seeds in late summer or in fall. **Special Care:** Keep on pebble tray to increase humidity. Keep away from drafts. Aphids may be a problem.

**CALLISIA elegans** (Striped Inch Plant)

The leaves of the striped inch plant are pinstriped green and white on top with deep purple undersides. Tiny white flowers sometimes appear on particularly happy plants. This easy-to-grow plant looks best when it is pinched regularly and given good light and water; otherwise, the long trailing stems can become straggly.

**Light:** Bright indirect or curtain-filtered light. **Water:** Keep soil moist but not soggy. **Temperature:** Normal room temperatures. **Soil:** Standard potting mix. **Fertilization:** Feed monthly from spring through fall. **Propagation:** Take tip cuttings. **Special Care:** Stems become straggly and bare with age, but if underwatered or given insufficient light, will loose lower leaves prematurely. Cut back to encourage new growth. Leaves loose stripes in low light.

**CALLISTEMON citrinus** (Bottlebrush)

The long feathery flower stalks of this intriguing plant look just like bottlebrushes. These brushes tip every stem all summer long and the plant begins blooming at an early age. Surprisingly, because it is not commonly grown, the bottlebrush blooms readily indoors—just give it plenty of sun and observe its need for a dormant period.

**Light:** Full sun. **Water:** Keep soil moist during growing season. Allow soil to dry somewhat during dormancy. **Temperature:** Normal room temperatures during growth. A winter dormancy of 45°F (7°C) is essential. **Soil:** Standard potting mix. **Fertilization:** Feed monthly during growing season. **Propagation:** Take stem cuttings in spring. Use rooting hormone and keep warm. **Special Care:** Prune back severely in early spring to keep compact. Tolerates low humidity.

**CAMPANULA isophylla** (Italian Bellflower)
When in bloom, from midsummer through fall, the Italian bellflower makes a colorful splash. Grow it in a hanging basket where the trailing stems will create a graceful mound covered with blue or white blossoms. 'Alba' is the most common variety and bears white flowers. It is easier to grow than the blue-flowered 'Mayi' (top) which requires more warmth.
**Light:** Bright indirect or curtain-filtered southern exposure. **Water:** Keep soil moist during the growing season. **Temperature:** Normal room temperatures except in winter when cool night temperatures are needed. **Soil:** Standard potting mix. **Fertilization:** Feed monthly during growth. **Propagation:** Take stem cuttings in spring. **Special Care:** Keep cool, on the dry side, and out of direct sun during the winter.

**CAPSICUM annuum** (Christmas Pepper, Ornamental Pepper)
It's the glossy pointed fruits and not the flowers that give this plant its colorful appeal. The small upright peppers ripen from green to white to yellow and finally to red, and are edible—though extremely hot. Usually purchased in fall when the fruits are ripening, the Christmas pepper will remain showy for months, but should be discarded after the fruits drop since the plant is an annual and will not bloom or produce fruits another time.
**Light:** Give four hours of direct sun each day. **Water:** Keep soil moist. **Temperature:** Normal room temperatures. **Soil:** Do not repot. **Fertilization:** Needs no food if bought while fruiting. **Propagation:** Started from seeds at the nursery; difficult to grow at home. **Special Care:** Whiteflies may be a problem.

**CATHARANTHUS roseus** (Rose Periwinkle)
The glossy green foliage of the rose periwinkle is pretty enough alone, but it is constantly capped with perky flowers to further add to its appeal. The five-petaled blossoms, either white or rose, have a dark rose or red eye in their centers. Rose periwinkle is sometimes listed as *Vinca rosea*.
**Light:** Provide an eastern or curtain-filtered southern exposure for maximum bloom. **Water:** Keep soil moist and do not allow soil ball to dry out. **Temperature:** Normal room temperatures are fine. **Soil:** Standard potting mix. **Fertilization:** Apply fertilizer once a month. **Propagation:** Started from seed at the nursery. Stem cuttings may be taken anytime. **Special Care:** Keep out of burning noon sun. Average humidity.

**CEPHALOCEREUS senilis** (Old-Man Cactus)
This curious specimen of a cactus resembles a big ball of lint more than it does a cactus. The long silvery hairs completely cover the gray-green stem and hide the sharp yellow spines. In the Mexican desert, where the old-man cactus is native, the hair acts to shade the plant. As a houseplant it grows the most hairs when it is given full sun.
**Light:** At least four hours of direct sun a day. **Water:** Allow soil to dry somewhat between waterings during summer. Water once a month during winter. **Temperature:** Normal room temperatures are acceptable during growth; needs nights about 45°F (7°C) in winter. **Soil:** Use standard cactus/succulent mix. **Fertilization:** Apply bone meal once each spring. **Propagation:** By seed. **Special Care:** Rotate to keep hair growth even and stem growth straight. Houseplants do not bloom.

**CEREUS** (Peruvian Apple Cactus, Curiosity Plant)
These green or blue-green cacti grow into tall, branched treelike forms. Rapid growers, they bloom when mature, producing slightly fragrant funnel-shaped flowers that last only one night. *C. peruvianus*, the Peruvian apple cactus, is named after its edible applelike fruits. Its variety 'Monstrosus' (middle) is a mutant that grows very slowly forming many-branched knobs.
**Light:** Needs at least four hours of direct sun each day. **Water:** Allow soil to dry somewhat between waterings during growth; water monthly in winter. **Temperature:** Normal room temperatures; night temperatures about 45°F (7°C) in winter are best. **Soil:** Use standard cactus/succulent mix. **Fertilization:** Apply bone meal once each spring. **Propagation:** Stem cuttings taken in spring. **Special Care:** Rots if overwatered.

**CEROPEGIA** (String-of-Hearts, Rosary Vine, Heart Vine)
This fascinating succulent has heart-shaped leaves that are marbled green and silver. Curious purple flowers appear in fall and by midwinter change into seedpods that burst open, releasing milkweedlike seeds. String-of-hearts is best displayed in a hanging basket where the dainty leaves can dangle freely from the thin trailing stems.
**Light:** Grows best in bright indirect light, but tolerates some direct sun. **Water:** Allow soil to dry between waterings. **Temperature:** Normal room temperatures. **Soil:** Cactus/succulent mix. **Fertilization:** Feed every two weeks with half-strength fertilizer. **Propagation:** Stem cuttings taken anytime. Remove bulbs that form along stem. **Special Care:** Prune straggly stems or cut back if too long; may grow to four feet.

### CHAMAEDOREA elegans (Parlor Palm)

This commonly-grown palm is popular for its decorative foliage as well as for its near-indestructibility. Often purchased as a small plant about six inches tall, it can grow to four feet in a few years or remain small, depending upon the amount of light and fertilizer it receives.

**Light:** Keep out of direct sun. Does best in bright indirect light; tolerates low light. **Water:** Keep soil moist. **Temperature:** Room temperatures are fine; cool winter nights are best. **Soil:** Standard potting mix. Repot only when very pot-bound. **Fertilization:** Feed monthly during growing season. **Propagation:** Seeds need warm temperature to germinate. **Special Care:** Mist in winter to discourage spider mites. Brown leaf tips are due to dry air. Lower leaves turn brown with age; cut off. Yellow leaves are due to underwatering.

### CHAMAEROPS humilis (European Fan Palm)

The stiff spreading leaves of this plant have sharp spines and arise from a rough trunk covered with black hairs. Older palms may have multiple trunks and are quite attractive and full. The European fan palm was a favorite plant during Victorian times.

**Light:** Does best with four hours of direct sun a day, but grows well with bright indirect light. **Water:** Keep soil very moist but not soggy during the growing season, a bit drier in winter. **Temperature:** Keep in a cool but frost-free place in winter; normal room temperatures the rest of the year. **Soil:** Use standard potting mix with dried cow manure added. **Fertilization:** Feed monthly from spring through fall. **Propagation:** May be divided in spring or propagated from seeds. **Special Care:** Needs a deep pot.

### CHLOROPHYTUM (Spider Plant, Airplane Plant)

Spider plants are loved for their habit of sending out skinny branches from the mother plant on which miniature spider plants dangle. These plantlets can be cut off and potted as separate plants or left to hang like spiders suspended from a web. White-striped varieties are the most popular, though solid green ones are also available.

**Light:** Bright indirect light; avoid direct sun. **Water:** Keep soil moist from spring through fall; allow to dry somewhat in winter. **Temperature:** Room temperatures. **Soil:** Standard potting mix. **Fertilization:** Feed monthly. **Propagation:** Root plantlets. **Special Care:** Closely follow cultural needs for best-looking plants. Cut off brown leaf tips, which are due to low humidity, underwatering, too much sun, or chemicals in tap water. Produces most plantlets when pot-bound.

## CHRYSANTHEMUM (Chrysanthemum, Mum)

The lovely potted mums that are available from florists throughout the year make a colorful display indoors for a month or so, but then should be discarded. They will not bloom indoors without special greenhouse conditions and even if planted outdoors, they probably will not live to bloom again, since most hothouse mums are not cold hardy. Enjoy them as temporary houseplants.

**Light:** Provide bright indirect light. **Water:** Keep soil moist. **Temperature:** Normal room temperatures. Flowers will last longest at cool temperatures. **Soil:** No need to repot. **Fertilization:** Not needed. **Propagation:** Cuttings from nonflowering stems will root and could be grown to flowering in a greenhouse. **Special Care:** Purchase plants whose flower buds are just beginning to open. Inspect for aphids. May plant outdoors where temperature does not fall below 20°F (−7°C) in winter.

## CISSUS (Kangaroo Vine, Grape Ivy)

The grape ivy (bottom), *(C. rhombifolia)*, and the kangaroo vine (middle), *(C. antarctica)*, are both vigorous vines with strong tendrils that will wrap around almost any kind of support. They are typically grown in hanging baskets, where the stems will cascade somewhat but often grow upwards and outwards in search of something to grasp. These vines can be grown on a trellis, where they will produce a pretty wall of foliage.

Grape ivy has three-lobed leaves whose undersides are covered with brown fuzz. It is an undemanding plant that adapts to almost any growing conditions—sun or shade and hot or cold temperatures—and isn't even particular about how it is watered. The kangaroo vine has undivided leaves with sawtooth edges. It is a bit more finicky, but still is not difficult to grow. Give it consistent care and it will thrive.

**Light:** Both do best in bright indirect light. Grape ivy tolerates some direct sun and low light. **Water:** Keep moist during the growing season; allow soil to dry somewhat between waterings in winter. **Temperature:** Keep at normal room temperatures, but cool winter temperatures are best. **Soil:** Use standard potting mix. **Fertilization:** Feed monthly from spring through fall. **Propagation:** Stem cuttings taken in spring or summer. **Special Care:** Mist occasionally and wash dust from leaves. Pinch stems to encourage branching. Brown shiny spots on leaves are due to too much direct sun. Curled leaves which drop off are due to low humidity. Wilting may be due to overwatering.

41

**CISSUS discolor** (Begonia Vine, Begonia Treebine)
This beautiful vine is not a begonia, but was so named because its silver-and-green foliage with maroon undersides resembles that of the rex begonias. It has twining tendrils and stems that are also maroon-colored. Unlike its relative grape ivy, the begonia vine is a delicate plant that is difficult to grow. It demands high humidity and warm temperatures if it is to thrive.
**Light:** Bright indirect light. **Water:** Keep soil moist but not soggy. **Temperature:** Needs warmth; should not fall below 65°F (18°C) in winter. **Soil:** Standard potting mix. **Fertilization:** Feed monthly from spring through fall. **Propagation:** Take cuttings in spring or summer. **Special Care:** Needs high humidity. Pinch stems to encourage bushiness. Provide support for twining stems if climbing plant is desired.

**CITROFORTUNELLA mitis** (Calamondin Orange)
A hybrid of an orange and a kumquat, the calamondin orange is the easiest citrus plant to grow as a houseplant. It forms a small bush that flowers and produces fruit at an early stage. In fall and winter, the waxy fragrant white flowers appear and change into small round fruit that take many months to ripen from green to orange. The fruit may still be on the tree when the next flush of blossoms appears.
**Light:** Full sun all day from a southern exposure. **Water:** Allow soil to dry somewhat between waterings. **Temperature:** Keep cool during the winter, about 50°F (10°C) at night. **Soil:** Standard potting mix. **Fertilization:** Feed monthly. **Propagation:** Take stem cuttings in spring. Use rooting hormone. **Special Care:** Mist when flowering. If fruit fails to form, hand pollinate next flowers.

**CLERODENDRUM thomsoniae** (Glory-Bower)
When purchased, this tropical plant is usually a bushy specimen of dark green leaves and red-and-white flowers. But in your home it will soon reveal its true identity as a climber by sending out long, rapidly growing stems. Pruning and pinching will keep it compact, but if you have room, give it a trellis and allow it to climb. Blossoms appear in spring and summer on new growth.
**Light:** Very bright indirect light. **Water:** Keep moist from spring through fall. Allow to dry somewhat in winter. **Temperature:** Normal home conditions; about 50°F (10°C) during December and January. **Soil:** Standard potting mix. **Fertilization:** Feed monthly during growth. **Propagation:** Take stem cuttings. **Special Care:** Needs high humidity. Does best in a greenhouse. Cut back severely in spring.

42

**CLEYERA japonica** (Cleyera, Sakaki)

The new leaves of this foliage plant emerge a deep brownish red, a beautiful contrast to the mature glossy green leaves with their red midribs. The variety 'Tricolor' (top) has yellow and green leaves which are rose-tinted when young. Small fragrant blossoms appear on the green-leaved variety in fall and are followed by red berries.

**Light:** Bright indirect light. **Water:** Keep soil moist. **Temperature:** Cool room temperatures. Needs 50°F (10°C) during winter. **Soil:** Use standard potting mix with extra peat. **Fertilization:** Feed monthly during growing season with acid-type fertilizer. **Propagation:** Stem cuttings in spring need rooting hormone. **Special Care:** This finicky plant likes high humidity and suffers in hot weather. Keep on a pebble tray. Pinch stems to encourage a bushy shape.

**CLIVIA miniata** (Clivia, Kaffir Lily)

The bold orange, scarlet, or yellow flowers of this relative of the amaryllis are a beautiful sight from December through April. Unlike the amaryllis, the Kaffir lily is evergreen. However, it does require a dormant period in late fall. Without dormancy, the plant will not bloom.

**Light:** Bright indirect light. **Water:** Keep moist from the time flower stalks are six inches tall until late autumn; during dormancy give only enough water to keep foliage from wilting. **Temperature:** Normal home conditions; about 55°F (13°C) during dormancy. **Soil:** Use standard potting mix with dried manure added. Repot only in spring when very crowded. **Fertilization:** Feed monthly during growing season. **Propagation:** Divide bulbs when repotting. **Special Care:** Must have dormant period.

**CODIAEUM variegatum** (Croton)

Crotons are the most vividly colored of all houseplants. Their variously shaped foliage can be patterned with red, bronze, purple, gold, pink, ivory, or green in blotches or spots, along the veins, or covering the entire leaf surface. And individual leaves on the same plant often exhibit different colors and patterns.

**Light:** Direct morning sun is best; bright indirect light is acceptable. **Water:** Keep moist from spring through fall; allow to dry slightly in winter. **Temperature:** Prefers warm temperatures, nights above 60°F (16°C). Avoid cold or hot drafts. **Soil:** Standard potting mix. **Fertilization:** Feed once in spring and once in summer. **Propagation:** Take cuttings or air-layer. **Special Care:** Lack of soil moisture or sudden temperature changes cause lower leaves to drop. Needs humid air.

43

### CODONANTHE (Codonanthe)

A member of the gesneriad family, codonanthe is less commonly grown than the African violet and the lipstick plant, two popular members of the same family. Its foliage and vining stems are slightly succulent, and it produces tubular blossoms with widely flared lips along the length of the stems. These blossoms may be white or pinkish and the tubes are often red-spotted. **Light:** Bright indirect light. Avoid direct summer sun. **Water:** Allow soil to dry somewhat between waterings. **Temperature:** Prefers warmth. Normal room temperatures are acceptable. Winter night temperature should not drop below 60°F (16°C). **Soil:** Use standard gesneriad mix. **Fertilization:** Apply monthly. **Propagation:** Take stem cuttings in spring. **Special Care:** Plant in a hanging basket. Pinch and prune to keep trailing stems in bounds.

### COFFEA arabica (Coffee Plant)

Only when it is mature and about six feet tall will the coffee plant, when grown as a houseplant, produce flowers and coffee beans. But until then, it will be admired for its glossy green leaves, which are wavy-edged and quite attractive. Pruning and pinching keeps the plant compact and also encourages it to form multiple trunks and a bushy shape. **Light:** Needs bright indirect light. **Water:** Keep soil very moist but not soggy. **Temperature:** Normal room temperatures. Winter nights should not drop below 50°F (10°C). **Soil:** Standard potting mix. **Fertilization:** Feed monthly. **Propagation:** Take stem cuttings in spring; use rooting hormone. Unroasted coffee beans germinate if given warmth. **Special Care:** Prefers a moderate to high humidity. Keep away from drafts.

### COLEUS (Coleus, Painted Nettle)

The modern coleus is a miracle of plant breeding. A dull-looking plant in its native Javan habitat, thanks to modern science coleus now comes in an assortment of color schemes combining green with cream, maroon, pink, red, orange and yellow-green. Its leaves can be lance-shaped or have crinkled or ruffled edges. When the plants get old and unattractive, simply renew them from cuttings. **Light:** A half day of direct morning sun is best; all-day sun may bleach leaf colors. Leaf colors may be too dull in low light. **Water:** Keep soil moist. **Temperature:** Normal room temperatures. **Soil:** Standard potting mix. **Fertilization:** Feed once a month. **Propagation:** Take cuttings anytime. **Special Care:** Pinch and prune stems to promote branching. Remove flower buds to prolong this annual's life.

## COLUMNEA (Columnea, Goldfish Plant)

Columnea is one of the most demanding of the hanging-basket gesneriads, but also the most rewarding if you grow it correctly. Literally covered with tubular scarlet, yellow, or orange flowers from winter through spring, it makes a stunning sight when in bloom. The blossoms have two lips; the lower one is deeply cut and flared, and the upper one forms a hood, giving the blossoms the appearance of goldfish tails.

The tricky part about growing columneas is providing sufficient humidity and a cool dormant period. If these two requirements are not met, the plants fail to bloom. A greenhouse is the best solution, but a humidified room will do.

*C. banksii* (top) does fairly well in the home. It has waxy leaves and scarlet flowers faintly striped with yellow. *Columnea microphylla* (middle) comes in a green-leaved or a variegated-leaved form. Its blossoms are scarlet with a yellow blotch and the leaves are hairy. *C. schiedeana* produces yellow flowers with maroon spots. Many hybrids are available.

**Light:** Bright indirect light. **Water:** Keep moist from the time flower buds first appear until late autumn; then allow soil to dry somewhat between waterings. **Temperature:** Normal room temperatures, except in dormancy when nights should drop to 50°F (10°C). **Soil:** Standard gesneriad mix. **Fertilization:** Feed every two weeks during growing season. **Propagation:** Take cuttings in spring. **Special Care:** Keep humidity high. Cut back stems to several inches in spring; flowers form only on new growth. Provide dormant period.

## CONOPHYTUM (Cone Plant, Living Stone)

These curious succulents adapted to life in the desert by mimicking rocks and pebbles. Each plant has a single pair of fat fleshy leaves that are joined together to form a cone with a "window" in the center. Their surfaces are waxy green or gray-green and marbled or spotted with dark green, purple, or brown. An astonishing contrast to the plant itself, the flowers are beautiful daisylike blooms of yellow, magenta, or white.

**Light:** Bright indirect light or morning sun. **Water:** Allow soil to dry somewhat between waterings from June through November. Water lightly once or twice in winter and spring. **Temperature:** Room temperatures during growth; cool, down to 40°F (4°C), in winter. **Soil:** Cactus/succulent mix. Repot every three years. **Fertilization:** Do not fertilize. **Propagation:** Divide clumps in spring when growth resumes. **Special Care:** Needs low humidity.

## CORDYLINE (Ti Plant, Hawaiian Ti, Good-Luck Plant, Cabbage Tree, Grass Palm)

These popular foliage plants closely resemble the dracaenas and indeed they were once classified in the same genus. Cordylines can easily be distinguished from dracaenas because their roots are white inside, and those of dracaenas are yellow.

The ti plant (top and middle), *C. terminalis,* is noted for its colorful leaves that are often streaked or spotted with pink or red. 'Tricolor' is the most colorful variety—its foliage is green with pink, red and creamy white variegations along the edges. 'Amabilis' offers glossy green leaves spotted with rose and white, and 'Baptisii' has leaves striped with pink and yellow.

The ti plant is often sold as a novelty plant that can be grown from a dried-up piece of stem. Simply plant the cane cutting horizontally a few inches beneath the soil surface and foliage pops up in a matter of weeks.

The cabbage tree, *C. australis,* grows into a small treelike plant with tall slender stems and a tuft of spreading grassy leaves on top. 'Atropurpurea' has foliage marked with purple midribs and 'Douchetii' has white-edged leaves.

**Light:** Four hours of direct light produce the best foliage colors in the ti plant; bright indirect light is acceptable for the ti plant and the cabbage tree. **Water:** Keep soil moist during growth; allow to dry somewhat in winter. **Temperature:** Normal room temperatures; not below 60°F (16°C) in winter. **Soil:** Standard potting mix. **Fertilization:** Feed every two months from spring through fall. **Propagation:** Take cane cuttings or air-layer. **Special Care:** Needs high humidity. Lower leaves drop with age and will fall prematurely if plant is underwatered or exposed to cold drafts.

## COTYLEDON (Silver-Crown, Silver-Ruffles)

These shrublike succulents boast tightly clustered flat leaves which are covered with a fine white dusting of fuzz. *C. orbiculata,* the silver-crown, is widely grown and can become quite large. Closely resembling it is silver-ruffles (bottom), *C. undulata,* with undulating leaf margins that further add to its appeal. Both produce clusters of orange-red flowers.

**Light:** Four hours of direct sun. **Water:** Let soil dry somewhat between waterings during growth. Allow to dry thoroughly during dormancy. **Temperature:** Normal room temperatures. **Soil:** Cactus/succulent mix. **Fertilization:** Feed every two weeks during growth with half-strength high-phosphorus fertilizer. **Propagation:** Cuttings of new growth. **Special Care:** May grow during winter and rest during summer, but can adapt to reverse cycle.

46

**CRASSULA** (Jade Plant, Silver-Dollar, Propeller Plant, String-of-Buttons)

This diverse group of succulents offers a host of interesting plants for a sunny windowsill. The popular jade plant (bottom), *C. argentea,* is the most well known of the group. Its fleshy green leaves are arranged in pairs along thick stems that can become quite woody with age. If pinched and pruned, the jade plant grows into a pleasingly symmetrical small shrub. Several varieties of the jade plant are available with variegated foliage—marked with white, yellow, or rosy hues.

Similar in size and shape is the silver-dollar plant, *C. arborescens,* noted for its gray-white leaves with red margins. This outstanding-looking plant makes a beautiful contrast to green-leaved houseplants. The propeller plant, *C. falcata* (middle), is noted for its odd, symmetrical leaf arrangement. Its gray-green sickle-shaped leaves are arranged in a single rank and remind one of propeller blades. Another favorite is string-of-buttons (top), *C. perforata.* It's a semi-creeping plant whose pairs of rounded leaves appear to be pierced by the stem, like a button by thread.

Though crassulas produce large clusters of tiny flowers outdoors, indoors they are reluctant to bloom. The propeller plant may produce red flowers if its cultural requirements are closely adhered to.

**Light:** Four hours of direct sunlight or curtain-filtered southern exposure are best. May do well in very bright indirect light. **Water:** Allow soil to dry somewhat between waterings from spring through summer; allow to dry thoroughly between waterings in fall and winter. **Temperature:** Normal room temperatures during growing season. Does best with a cool period in winter. **Soil:** Standard cactus/succulent mix, or a mixture of half potting soil and half sand. **Fertilization:** Feed twice a month from spring through summer with half-strength high-phosphorus fertilizer. **Propagation:** Take stem cuttings from young growth; leaf cuttings will grow roots and then form tiny plants. Allow the cut surfaces of the cuttings to dry for several days before putting in rooting medium. **Special Care:** Prefers to be potbound. Grow in clay pots that are wider than deep. Foliage facing window can become sunburned if light is too strong. If insects are a problem, wash leaves with soapy water since crassulas are sensitive to insecticide. Allow leaves to dry before placing in sun, or foliage may be injured.

47

**CROSSANDRA** (Crossandra, Firecracker Plant)
Admired for its bright orange spikes of flowers, which appear above the gleaming green foliage from spring through fall, the firecracker plant is difficult to grow as a houseplant. It must have high humidity and this is difficult to achieve without a greenhouse. If grouped with other plants on a pebble tray, the humidity may be sufficient to keep the firecracker plant happy.
**Light:** Bright indirect light. Avoid direct sun. **Water:** Keep soil moist. **Temperature:** Normal room temperatures. Should not drop below 55°F (13°C) in winter. **Soil:** Standard potting mix. **Fertilization:** Feed every two weeks from spring through fall. **Propagation:** Take cuttings in spring. **Special Care:** Provide high humidity. Prune severely in spring. Spider mites may be a problem. Yellow foliage is due to overwatering.

**CRYPTANTHUS** (Earth-Star, Starfish Plant, Rainbow-Star)
The multicolored foliage of these appealing bromeliads is arranged in a flattened rosette that resembles a star. Leaves are frequently colored with a rose flush, or striped or banded with color. Not very showy, the flowers are small and hidden among the leaves. After flowering, the rosette dies, but the "pups" that usually form alongside the main rosette will live on.

Several species are popular and make excellent houseplants if they can be kept warm enough in winter. *C. lacerdae* (middle) is a miniature plant called the silver-star because its leathery green leaves are marked with silver in their centers. Banded with zigzag patterns of light green, brown, or white, *C. zonatus* (bottom) is sometimes called the zebra plant. It's truly a remarkable-looking plant and its colors are most vibrant when it's given plenty of bright light.

*C. acaulis* is sometimes called the starfish plant. This small plant has many varieties that are pink or rose tinted. All have undulating leaf margins bearing sharp spines. Sometimes confused with it is *C. bromelioides* 'Tricolor,' the rainbow-star. Its leaves are striped ivory and green and are flushed with rose.
**Light:** Bright indirect light. **Water:** Keep soil moist but not soggy. Do not pour water into the funnel. **Temperature:** Needs warmth. Days should be at least 70°F (21°C) and nights not colder than 60°F (16°C). **Soil:** Use standard bromeliad mix and a small pot, or mount on a bark slab. **Fertilization:** Feed monthly from spring through fall. **Propagation:** Divide offsets from parent rosette. **Special Care:** Needs high humidity and warmth. Avoid direct sun.

## CTENANTHE (Never-Never Plant)

This stunning foliage plant is larger growing and a bit more tricky to cultivate than its relative the prayer plant. The long-stemmed oblong leaves are marbled between the veins with yellow, cream, or dark green and the undersides are often tinted wine-red. Adhere closely to its cultural requirements and the never-never plant will grow into a lush and impressive two- or three-foot-tall specimen.

**Light:** Bright indirect light. **Water:** Keep soil moist but not soggy. **Temperature:** Needs warmth; not below 65°F (18°C) in winter. **Soil:** Standard potting mix with extra peat. **Fertilization:** Feed monthly from spring through fall. **Propagation:** Divide plant in spring. **Special Care:** Grow on pebble tray and group with other plants to keep humidity high. Keep out of direct sun.

## CUPHEA ignea (Cigar Flower)

The cigar flower gets its name from its slender red flowers complete with ash-gray tips, which nod from its thin stems all summer long. Varieties of the cigar flower offer other flower colors—white, purple, rose and pink. Blooms are most profuse on young plants, so it is best to renew the plant each year from cuttings taken in spring after the winter rest period.

**Light:** At least four hours of direct sun each day. **Water:** Keep soil moist; allow to dry somewhat in winter. **Temperature:** Normal room temperatures, except in winter when 50°F (10°C) nights are desirable. **Soil:** Standard potting mix. **Fertilization:** Feed every two weeks from spring through fall with half-strength fertilizer. **Propagation:** Take stem cuttings in spring. **Special Care:** Give winter dormancy.

## CYCLAMEN persicum (Cyclamen, Persian Violet)

The cyclamen features beautiful blossoms with back-swept petals that nod above heart-shaped leaves. Flowers are white, pink, salmon, fuchsia, red, or purple with a contrasting eye. The leaves are usually marbled with silver or light green. Cyclamen blooms nonstop from fall through spring.

**Light:** Bright indirect light or a north window. **Water:** Keep moist. Do not wet crown. **Temperature:** Needs temperatures between 50° and 60°F (10° and 16°C) during flowering. **Soil:** Standard potting mix. **Fertilization:** Feed monthly. **Propagation:** Sow seeds in summer. **Special Care:** Grow on pebble tray. Yellow foliage is due to hot, dry air. Twisted foliage is due to cyclamen mite; destroy plant. After flowering, allow to go dormant by placing in cool, dim place and withholding water. Replant tuber in late summer.

## CYMBIDIUM (Cymbidium)

The miniature varieties of the cymbidium are some of the best orchids for houseplant culture. The grasslike foliage stays about a foot tall, but bears spikes of up to thirty three-inch flowers in winter or spring.

**Light:** Provide four hours of direct morning sun. Avoid hot noon sun. **Water:** Keep moist from spring through fall; water only enough to keep from shriveling in winter. **Temperature:** Needs days of at least 68°F (20°C) and nights between 50° and 60°F (10° and 16°C). **Soil:** Use standard orchid bark-mixture. **Fertilization:** Feed every two weeks from spring through fall with high-nitrogen food, with low-nitrogen food thereafter. **Propagation:** Divide in spring. **Special Care:** Leaves should be yellow-green. Dark green-leaved plants need more sun.

## CYPERUS (Umbrella Plant, Sedge, Papyrus)

These may be the only houseplants you can't overwater! In fact, umbrella plants must be kept constantly wet because they are bog plants. They grow as clumps of thin stems topped by narrow leaves that radiate from the stems like the spokes of an umbrella. Grasslike flower heads often form among the leaves.

*C. alternifolius* (middle) is a popular plant that also makes a good houseplant. It grows to about three feet tall, but its dwarf variety 'Gracilis,' which grows half as tall, is more suitable to indoor culture. 'Variegatus' has green leaves striped with white. Also small-sized and suitable for a houseplant is the mini-papyrus (bottom), *C. isocladus.*

**Light:** A few hours of direct sun is best, but avoid hot noon sun. Both dim light and bright indirect light are acceptable. **Water:** Keep pot standing in a saucer of water. **Temperature:** Normal room temperatures are acceptable. **Soil:** Use a mixture of one-third potting soil, one-third peat, and one-third sand. May also be grown in water. Repot every spring. **Fertilization:** Feed weekly with quarter-strength fertilizer. **Propagation:** Divide plants in spring, keeping outer plants and discarding older, center ones. May also be propagated by cuttings made from the leaf crown and about two inches of stem. Float these in water. **Special Care:** Do not let soil dry out. Mist occasionally. Cut out yellowing stems to improve plant's vigor. Will resprout new foliage if foliage is cut back severely in spring. Brown leaf tips are due to dry air or soil. Spider mites may be a problem if humidity is low.

50

## CYRTOMIUM falcatum (Holly Fern)

This leathery-leaved beauty is one of the best ferns for beginners because it tolerates a wide range of conditions. The fronds are made up of many leaflets that may be smooth-edged, but are often toothed like a holly leaf. The arching fronds of a well-grown plant can reach two feet long.

**Light:** Does best in bright indirect light, but tolerates both brighter and dimmer light. **Water:** Keep soil moist but not soggy. **Temperature:** Normal room temperatures, though cool winter nights are preferred. **Soil:** Standard potting mix. **Fertilization:** Feed monthly from spring through fall. **Propagation:** May be divided in spring or propagated from spores. **Special Care:** Wash leaves when dusty. Misting is not necessary. Cut off old yellowing leaves. Deformed leaves are due to low light.

## CYTISUS (Broom)

In spring, broom produces long spikes of yellow pealike blossoms on the tips of its branches. The rest of the year it makes a fine-textured foliage plant. A difficult plant to grow in a heated home, broom is often sold in bloom by florists as a gift plant.

**Light:** Full sun in summer; may be kept outdoors. Bright indirect light the remainder of the year. **Water:** Keep moist except in fall when should be allowed to dry somewhat. **Temperature:** During resting period, keep between 40° and 50°F (5° and 10°C). **Soil:** Standard potting mix. **Fertilization:** Feed monthly in spring and summer. **Propagation:** Take cuttings in spring or summer. **Special Care:** Keep in cool, frost-free place from September to January. Then return to warm, bright conditions to induce bloom.

## DATURA (Angel's-Trumpet)

The angel's-trumpet produces huge creamy funnel-shaped blossoms that dangle from its branches during the summer. This plant is difficult to grow as a houseplant because it is so large, needs such a cool resting period, and needs so much sun during the growing season. It is however suitable for a sunporch or a greenhouse.

**Light:** Full sun from spring through fall. Bright indirect light in winter. **Water:** Keep moist during growing season; allow to dry somewhat during dormancy. **Temperature:** Warm temperatures; 45°F (7°C) during rest. **Soil:** Standard potting mix. Repot each spring into large container. **Fertilization:** Feed weekly during growth with quarter-strength plant food. **Propagation:** Take cuttings in spring. **Special Care:** Cut back in spring. Needs cool dormant period in winter.

51

## DIDYMOCHLAENA truncatula (Didymochlaena)

This tropical fern needs a tropical environment to do really well. If you can keep it in a warm and humid place (a greenhouse is ideal), it will prosper and reward you with a full crown of twice-divided dark green fronds.

**Light:** Bright indirect light or a north window. **Water:** Keep soil moist from spring through fall. Allow to dry somewhat between waterings in winter. **Temperature:** Warm room temperatures. **Soil:** Standard potting mix. **Fertilization:** Feed every two weeks with quarter-strength fertilizer. **Propagation:** Divide in spring. **Special Care:** In October, move to cool location, do not feed, and reduce watering until February. Then cut fronds back to several inches in length. New growth will sprout and should be misted several times a day until mature. Keep on pebble tray.

## DIEFFENBACHIA (Dumb Cane)

These handsome foliage plants are grown for their shiny bold-textured foliage, which can be marked or speckled with cream, white, yellow, or light green. *D. amoena* 'Tropic Snow' (middle) is a popular variety because of its beautiful markings and because the thick leaves are more resistant to low humidity than other varieties. *D. bausei* (bottom) is also a sturdy plant, as is *D. maculata*, the spotted dumb cane. Many other species and varieties are available.

These houseplants are a bit more tricky to grow than their popularity warrants. Unless given moderately high humidity and warm temperatures, a dumb cane can turn into a tall bare trunk with a few yellowing and brown-edged leaves on top. The sap from the foliage and trunk is poisonous if eaten and can irritate the skin if contact is prolonged.

**Light:** Leaf markings are best in bright indirect light; survives in low light. Avoid direct sun. **Water:** Allow soil to dry somewhat between waterings. **Temperature:** Needs warmth; does best when winter temperatures do not drop below 65°F (18°C). **Soil:** Standard potting mix. **Fertilization:** Feed monthly from spring through fall. **Propagation:** The tops of tall, leggy plants can be cut off and rooted, and cane cuttings can be made from the stem sections. A plant cut back to a four-inch stub will sprout new foliage. Plants may also be air-layered. **Special Care:** Wash dust from leaves. Needs moderately high humidity; group with other plants or grow in a humidified room. Lower leaves will turn yellow and drop from low humidity, low temperatures and cold drafts. Cut back or air-layer old leggy plants.

52

**DIPLADENIA** (Dipladenia)

If you can provide enough humidity for this tropical vine, it will reward you with masses of trumpet-shaped blossoms. The silky flowers come in shades of pink, rose and white. *D. sanderi* 'Rosea' is the best for home culture and it blooms throughout the year. Other varieties need more humidity and blossom only in summer.

**Light:** Bright indirect or curtain-filtered light; no direct sun. **Water:** Keep soil moist in growing season, drier in winter. **Temperature:** Warm temperatures, except in winter when 55° to 60°F (13° to 16°C) is needed at night. **Soil:** Standard potting mix. **Fertilization:** Feed every two weeks from spring through fall. **Propagation:** Take stem cuttings in spring; use rooting hormone. **Special Care:** Provide support for twining vines. Needs high humidity, especially when flowering.

**DIPTERACANTHUS devosiana** (Trailing Velvet Plant)

The velvety leaves of this tropical plant are marked with white veins and purple undersides. Slender white blossoms flushed with lavender appear throughout the year. This pretty plant is difficult to grow outside a greenhouse since it requires high humidity and warmth, but it may do well in a terrarium. It is sometimes listed in the genus *Ruellia*.

**Light:** Bright indirect light or low light. **Water:** Keep soil moist. **Temperature:** Needs warmth; not below 60°F (16°C). **Soil:** Standard potting mix with extra peat. **Fertilization:** Feed once a month during growing season. **Propagation:** Take stem cuttings in spring or summer. **Special Care:** Needs high humidity. Pinch back drastically in spring or renew from cuttings if plant becomes leggy.

**DIZYGOTHECA elegantissima** (False Aralia, Thread-Leaf)

Even a many-branched five-foot-tall false aralia has an airy grace to it because its leaves are so lacy. Made up of linear leaves with serrated edges, the foliage is often coppery colored or so dark green that it appears black. This tropical plant is a bit finicky, but will thrive if given consistently good care.

**Light:** Bright indirect or curtain-filtered light. **Water:** Keep moist but not soggy. **Temperature:** Likes warmth; not below 60°F (16°C) in winter. **Soil:** Standard potting mix. **Fertilization:** Feed monthly during the growing season. **Propagation:** Take cuttings from mature wood; use rooting hormone. **Special Care:** Needs moderately high humidity. Lower leaves will drop from low humidity, dry soil, or a cold draft.

## DRACAENA (Dracaena, Corn Plant, Dragon Tree)

Dracaenas are both decorative and durable! Many species and varieties are grown and they all make wonderful large floor plants, especially where a tree is needed to complete the decor of a room. For this reason, dracaenas are often used in offices and public buildings, but they are equally attractive in a home, where their graceful trunks topped with tufts of broad or grassy leaves go well with modern furnishings. Since dracaenas tolerate low light, they'll flourish even in interior spots away from a window where many other plants would languish.

Dracaenas are often purchased as large plants three or four feet tall—they can grow to six feet or more—with three trunks of different heights in one pot. Smaller plants are also sold and if you give them the proper culture and are patient, they will grow into impressive specimens. The small ones make becoming tabletop plants. When they get too tall for a table, you can cut them back—the bare trunk will sprout new leaves—or you can move them to a suitable spot on the floor.

Several different species, each looking quite unlike the others, are cultivated and all are very popular. *D. deremensis* has long, stiff swordlike leaves that are frequently striped with white. The most popular white-striped variety is 'Warneckii.' 'Bausei' and 'Longii' have leaves with central stripes. 'Janet Craig' is a popular variety with broad dark green leaves. This dracaena can grow to ten feet tall indoors, but should be cut back if it becomes too ungainly. Both 'Janet Craig' and 'Warneckii' come in slow-growing compact versions, which are good choices where a very large plant is unsuitable.

The dragon tree, *D. draco*, can grow very tall as well. Its broad green foliage is stiff and upright compared to other dracaenas. Also called the dragon tree, *D. marginata* is a more graceful-looking plant. Its long, narrow leaves are bordered with a thin band of reddish purple and arch gracefully downward. With age, the lower leaves drop and the plant resembles a palm tree with a gray trunk and a crown of foliage.

With much broader leaves and a thicker trunk, the corn plant, *D. fragrans*, makes a bold statement when used as a floor plant. Its most popular variety is 'Massangeana,' which has a golden central stripe on its leaves. 'Knerkii' lacks variegation and is colored grassy green. 'Lindenii' offers white borders and 'Victoria' offers golden borders on their leaves.

Pictured on this page: *Dracaena deremensis* (top), *D. draco* (middle) and *D. fragrans* (bottom).

54

Of all the dracaenas, *D. reflexa* branches most easily. This species readily forms side shoots and doesn't need to be cut back to encourage bushiness. While young, it is a full, leafy plant; with age, as with other dracaenas, the lower leaves drop and reveal the trunk. Many varieties of *D. reflexa* are cultivated. 'Song of India' is beautifully variegated with wide yellow margins. Other varieties are striped with light green.

The only popular dracaena that maintains a bushy shape and has broad leaves is the gold-dust dracaena, *D. surculosa*, which is also called *D. godseffiana*. Its oval leaves are spotted with gold when young. With age the spots fade to bright white. The variety 'Florida Beauty' is heavily spotted and is the most widely grown. The gold-dust dracaena grows more slowly than other dracaenas and eventually becomes a bushy two-and-a-half-foot specimen.

**Light:** Bright indirect light is best. A position close to a north window or several feet back from an east or a west window is fine if the plant is out of direct sun. Low light in an interior setting is acceptable, but the plant will grow very slowly. **Water:** Soil should be moist but not soggy and should never be allowed to dry out. Watering a dracaena properly is tricky, and plants are frequently killed by overwatering, or made unattractive by underwatering. **Temperature:** Normal room temperatures both in summer and winter are fine. Dracaenas do not need a cool dormant period. Most species prefer warmth, though they will not be harmed by temperatures of 55°F (13°C). *D. draco* can even tolerate temperatures down to 45°F (7°C) with no ill-effects. **Soil:** Use standard potting mix. Repot young plants annually and older plants every three years. Tolerates being slightly pot-bound. **Fertilization:** Feed monthly from spring through fall with half-strength fertilizer. **Propagation:** The top of a large dracaena may be air-layered and the remaining bare trunk can be cut back to four inches. The trunk will sprout one or two tufts of leaves and may then grow into a branched specimen. Pieces of trunk can be made into cane cuttings and planted horizontally below the soil surface to grow into young trunkless plants. **Special Care:** Dracaenas need moderate to high humidity. Low humidity will cause brown tips or yellow edges on the foliage. Leaves with brown spots are due to underwatering. Bleached dry areas on foliage are due to too much sun. Cold drafts will cause leaves to yellow and lower leaves to drop prematurely.

Pictured on this page: *Dracaena surculosa* (top), *D. marginata* (middle) and *D. reflexa* (bottom).

## DUCHESNEA indica (Indian Strawberry)

The long, wiry stems of the Indian strawberry can be trained around a trellis or allowed to drape over the edge of a hanging basket. Either way, the pretty three-lobed leaves, tiny golden flowers and red fruits will be shown off to great effect. Blooms appear in spring and summer and are followed by tiny ·strawberrylike fruits. The fruits are neither poisonous nor tasty.

**Light:** Bright indirect light or some direct sun, but shield from noon sun. **Water:** Keep soil moist. **Temperature:** Room temperatures during the growing season; needs 45°F (7°C) in winter. **Soil:** Standard potting mix. **Fertilization:** Fertilize once a month in spring and summer. **Propagation:** Plant stem sections bearing rootlets. **Special Care:** Must have a winter cold period; keep in an unheated room.

## ECHEVERIA (Echeveria, Hen-and-Chickens)

The fleshy leaves of these succulents are tightly packed into rosettes that hug the ground or are set at the ends of thick stems. These rosettes are so geometrically perfect that they resemble sculptured flowers. Many species make excellent houseplants.

Though echeverias produce stalks of bell-shaped flowers in spring, they are grown primarily for their beautiful leaves, which come in an array of earth-tones. There are echeverias with green leaves and echeverias with deep purple leaves. Others have gray-green, white, bluish-green or steel-blue leaves, and still others can be covered with white fuzz or a waxy coating.

*E. harmsii* (middle) is one of the few popular kinds that is branched and upright. Most echeverias take the form of *E. secunda* (bottom) and they frequently produce many tiny rosettes around the base of the large one. This cluster of rosettes is the reason for the common name hen-and-chickens, since the baby rosettes are gathered about the mother rosette.

**Light:** At least four hours of direct sun a day. **Water:** Allow soil to dry between waterings during the growing season; in winter, water only enough to keep plants from shriveling. **Temperature:** Normal room temperatures during growth; needs 50° to 65°F (10° to 18°C) in winter. **Soil:** Standard cactus/succulent mix. **Fertilization:** Feed once in spring with half-strength fertilizer. **Propagation:** Young rosettes may be removed and rooted. Rosettes atop long stems may be cut off and rooted. Leaf cuttings will root and form new plants. Allow cuttings to dry before planting. **Special Care:** Echeverias will rot if overwatered or if water remains between the leaves.

**ECHINOCACTUS grusonii** (Golden Barrel Cactus)
Round as a ball and covered with long, sharp yellow
spines, the golden barrel cactus is both interesting and
attractive. It grows slowly to a diameter of three feet;
when it reaches two feet across, the plant produces
beautiful yellow flowers in spring.
**Light:** At least six hours of direct sun each day. **Water:**
Allow soil to dry between waterings from March
through September. In winter, water once or twice to
keep plant from shriveling. **Temperature:** Warm day
temperatures, but as cool as possible at night; down to
at least 50°F (10°C) in winter. **Soil:** Standard cactus/
succulent mix. **Fertilization:** Feed monthly in spring
with half-strength high-phosphorus fertilizer. **Propagation:** By seed. **Special Care:** Must have cold nights
in winter; keep on windowsill or in unheated room.

**ECHINOPSIS** (Sea-Urchin Cactus, Easter-Lily
Cactus)
These cacti produce enormous night-blooming flowers that are comically out of proportion to the small
globular plants. *E. eyriesii,* (middle) has dark brown
spines and becomes barrel-shaped with age. *E. multi-
plex,* the Easter-lily cactus, grows as a cluster of small
globes with long yellow spines and fragrant flowers.
**Light:** Four to six hours of direct sun a day. **Water:**
Allow soil to dry between waterings from spring
through fall; water once or twice in winter. **Temperature:** Normal room temperatures during growth; in
winter, 40° to 55°F (4° to 13°C) at night, and 65°F (18°C)
or colder during the day. **Soil:** Standard cactus/succu-
lent mix. **Fertilization:** Feed once in spring with high-
phosphorus fertilizer. **Propagation:** Remove offsets in
spring. **Special Care:** Needs cold winter rest to flower.

**EPIDENDRUM** (Buttonhole Orchid)
There are hundreds of species of these dainty orchids,
but only a few do well as houseplants. *E. fragrans*
grows as a small pseudobulb and produces fragrant
cream-colored flowers all summer. Forming tall cane-
like stems, *E. difforme* produces waxy, pale green flowers in winter.
**Light:** Give plants with pseudobulbs a southern exposure shaded from noon sun. Cane-forming kinds
need morning sun. **Water:** Allow ones with pseudobulbs to dry between waterings; keep cane-forming
kinds moist. **Temperature:** Warm room temperatures
during growth; 50°F (10°C) in winter. **Soil:** Grow cane-
forming plants in terrestrial orchid mix, others in fir
bark. **Fertilization:** Feed every two weeks during
growth. **Propagation:** Divide in spring. **Special Care:**
Too much sun turns leaves reddish.

## EPIPHYLLUM (Orchid Cactus)

These unusual cacti grow naturally as epiphytes clinging to the branches of jungle trees, so they are accustomed to shade and plenty of moisture. They are grown not for curiously thorny stems, but for the breathtaking flowers they produce. Dozens of huge silky blossoms appear in spring on mature plants. They are usually fragrant, and may open only at night or only during the day.

**Light:** Bright indirect light. **Water:** Keep moist during growth; allow to dry somewhat between waterings in winter. **Temperature:** Cool room temperatures; winter nights about 55°F (13°C). **Soil:** A mixture of one-half peat and one-half sand. **Fertilization:** Feed monthly from spring through summer with low-nitrogen fertilizer. **Propagation:** Root stem sections after flowering; let dry before planting. **Special Care:** Warm winter temperatures discourage flowering. Needs small pot.

## EPISCIA (Flame Violet)

Flame violets, relatives of the African violet, are grown for both their foliage and their flowers. Often variegated with unusual colors—pink, bronze, silver, or light green—the hairy oval leaves have sunken veins, which give them an appealing quilted look. Small tubular flowers in orange, scarlet, yellow, pink, or white bloom on the trailing stems all summer.

**Light:** Bright indirect or curtain-filtered light. **Water:** Keep soil moist. **Temperature:** Warm room temperatures, not below 60°F (16°C). **Soil:** Standard potting mix with extra peat. **Fertilization:** Feed monthly with high-phosphorus plant food. **Propagation:** Take stem cuttings anytime. **Special Care:** Needs high humidity. Grow in hanging basket. Cut back ungainly stems to encourage branching.

## ERICA (Heath)

These fine-textured flowering plants are usually bought as ornamental Thanksgiving or Christmas gifts. If kept very cool, they'll display their small bell-shaped flowers for several months, then are best discarded since they are unlikely to reflower.

**Light:** Bright indirect or curtain-filtered light. **Water:** Needs moist soil. **Temperature:** Keep between 40° and 55°F (4° and 13°C) when in flower. **Soil:** Standard potting mix with extra peat. **Fertilization:** If keeping plant after flowers fade, feed with fertilizer designed for acid-loving plants once a month from spring through fall. **Propagation:** Take stem cuttings and use rooting hormone. **Special Care:** Place in cool, humid location. If keeping plant, cut back in spring and place outdoors in shady spot for the summer.

**ESPOSTOA lanata** (Peruvian Old-Man, Cotton-Ball)
This cactus is covered with short silky white hairs through which peek sharp yellow spines. It grows into a columnar shape, may branch, and eventually reaches three feet tall. As a houseplant the Peruvian old-man cactus rarely produces its nocturnal white blossoms.
**Light:** Four to six hours of direct sun. **Water:** Allow soil to dry between waterings from spring through fall. Water once or twice in winter. **Temperature:** Normal room temperatures throughout the year are fine, though cooler winter nights are acceptable. **Soil:** Standard cactus/succulent mix. **Fertilization:** Feed monthly from spring through summer with high-phosphorus fertilizer. **Propagation:** Branches may be cut off, allowed to dry, then rooted. **Special Care:** Overwatering in winter will cause plant to rot.

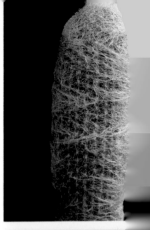

**EUGENIA paniculata** (Brush Cherry)
The needlelike leaves of the brush cherry emerge in a pretty bronze color before changing to bright green. Clusters of tiny white flowers and purple berries further add to its appeal. This airy plant has the feathery look of an asparagus fern, but since it's upright-growing, you can use it as a tub plant where an asparagus fern would be unsuitable. It needs cool winter temperatures, so try placing it in a brightly lit entranceway where more tender plants would fail.
**Light:** At least four hours of direct sun a day. **Water:** Keep soil moist. **Temperature:** Normal room temperatures; needs 55°F (13°C) at night in winter. **Soil:** Standard potting mix. **Fertilization:** Feed monthly from spring through fall. **Propagation:** Take stem cuttings in spring; sow seed when ripe. **Special Care:** Can be clipped into topiary shapes.

**EUONYMOUS japonica** (Euonymous)
Several variegated varieties of this glossy-leaved plant are popular houseplants. 'Aureomarginata' (bottom) has gold-edged foliage; 'Albomarginata' has narrow white-margined leaves. 'Aureovariegata' is adorned with a golden blotch in the middle of the leaves. Offering tiny white-edged foliage is 'Microphylla'. All need very cool winter temperatures—try them in an entranceway, an enclosed porch, or an unheated room.
**Light:** An eastern or western exposure. **Water:** Keep soil moist. **Temperature:** Normal room temperatures; needs 40° to 50°F (4° to 10°C) in winter. **Soil:** Standard potting mix. **Fertilization:** Feed once in spring and once in summer. **Propagation:** Take cuttings in spring. **Special Care:** Must have cool winters. Needs moderate humidity. Cut back and repot in spring.

59

### EUPHORBIA pulcherrima (Poinsettia)

Today, these traditional Christmas plants will festoon your home all winter since they are bred to last longer than ever before! The showy bracts, once available only in bright red, now also come in pink, salmon, white, cream, and variegated red and white, or pink and white. A poinsettia can be made to rebloom if you are skillful.

**Light:** Half a day of sun. **Water:** Keep moist. **Temperature:** Normal room temperatures. Avoid cold drafts. **Soil:** Standard potting mix. **Fertilization:** Feed every two weeks. **Propagation:** Take cuttings in spring. **Special Care:** To rebloom, cut back severely in spring and keep pinching until August. Beginning in September allow no more than ten hours of light each day on a consistent schedule—try putting the plant in a dark closet at 5:00 P.M. and removing it at 8:00 A.M.

### EUPHORBIA milii (Crown-of-Thorns)

The more light, water and sun you give it, the more leaves and flowers the crown-of-thorns produces. Let it dry out and the small oval leaves drop to reveal gray stems covered with very sharp thorns. Water it again and new foliage sprouts in a matter of days. Its dainty red or yellow flowers blossom throughout the year.

**Light:** At least four hours of direct sun. **Water:** Allow soil to dry somewhat between waterings; plant is tolerant of thorough drying, but is more attractive when watered regularly. **Temperature:** Normal room temperatures. **Soil:** Cactus/succulent mix. **Fertilization:** Feed once in spring and once in summer. **Propagation:** Take stem cuttings; allow cut surface to dry before planting. **Special Care:** To remove dried leaves, use point of a pencil to avoid sharp thorns.

### EUPHORBIA lophogona (Euphorbia, Spurge)

This very odd plant produces long waxy green leaves at the ends of its succulent stems. As the leaves fall off, they leave behind large scars on the branches, giving them a roughened texture. Small white or pink flowers appear in spring and change into black capsules. Seedlings of this euphorbia may pop up mysteriously out of neighboring pots because when the capsules are ripe, they burst open, shooting their seeds a great distance.

**Light:** Bright indirect light or some direct sun. **Water:** Allow soil to dry somewhat between waterings. Leaves drop off if soil dries thoroughly, but will regrow. **Temperature:** Normal room temperatures. **Soil:** Cactus/succulent mix. **Fertilization:** Feed once in spring and once in summer. **Propagation:** Sow seeds when ripe. **Special Care:** Tolerates low humidity.

**EUPHORBIA grandicornis** (Cow's-Horn)

At first glance, certain species of *Euphorbia* seem to resemble cactus since they have leafless thickened green stems and sharp thorns. One foolproof way to tell them apart is to scratch the plant surface slightly—euphorbias exude a milky sap. The cow's horn is the most popular of these cactuslike euphorbias. It grows tiers of leafless green branches whose ribs are studded with brown thorns.

**Light:** At least four hours of direct sun a day. **Water:** Allow soil to dry between waterings. **Temperature:** Normal room temperatures with winter nights down to at least 65°F (18°C). **Soil:** Standard cactus/succulent mix. **Fertilization:** Feed once in spring. **Propagation:** Branches may be used as cuttings; allow to dry before planting. **Special Care:** Tolerates low humidity.

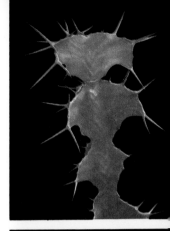

**EXACUM affine** (Persian Violet)

The perky blue, lavender, or white flowers of this plant make a delightful display from early summer well into fall. But once flowering ceases, even the heart-shaped leaves begin to wither, since the Persian violet is an annual and lives for only one year. You can renew it from cuttings in late summer, but it's best to simply enjoy the plant for its single season and then purchase a new one in spring.

**Light:** Bright indirect or curtain-filtered light. **Water:** Keep soil moist. **Temperature:** Cool room temperatures. **Soil:** Standard potting mix with extra peat. **Fertilization:** Feed every two weeks. **Propagation:** Usually started from seed in early spring; cuttings also may be made. **Special Care:** Pinch stems to create full plant. Remove faded blossoms to prolong flowering.

**FATSHEDERA lizei** (Tree Ivy, Botanical-Wonder)

This houseplant oddity is the result of an accidental hybridization between an ivy plant *(Hedera)* and a Japanese aralia *(Fatsia)*. The hybrid seedling was found in a nursery in France in 1910 and was quickly appreciated for its potential as a houseplant. Tree ivy has glossy five-lobed leaves like ivy, but they are huge like Japanese aralia. And it can be trained to climb like *Hedera* or be grown as an upright bushy plant like *Fatsia*. The variety 'Variegata' (bottom) has white-margined leaves.

**Light:** Bright indirect to low light. **Water:** Allow soil to dry somewhat between waterings. **Temperature:** Cool room temperatures. **Soil:** Standard potting mix. **Fertilization:** Feed monthly during growth. **Propagation:** Take cuttings in late summer. **Special Care:** Pinch tips to grow as a bush; provide support to grow as a vine.

61

**FATSIA japonica** (Japanese Aralia, Japanese Fatsia)
Japanese aralia grows quite rapidly into a four-foot-tall specimen that's a fabulous floor plant in a living room or hallway. The foliage is dark glossy green and deeply divided into five to nine lobes. The variety 'Variegata' has foliage with creamy-white markings. Japanese aralia is amazingly tolerant of unfavorable conditions. It is sometimes offered as *Aralia japonica*.

**Light:** Bright indirect light is best; tolerates some direct sun and low light. **Water:** Keep soil moist. **Temperature:** Cool room temperatures. **Soil:** Standard potting mix. **Fertilization:** Feed once in spring and once in summer. **Propagation:** Take cuttings in summer. **Special Care:** Spotted leaves or leaves with brown edges are due to overwatering. Brittle yellow leaves are due to low humidity.

**FAUCARIA** (Tiger-Jaws)
The paired triangular leaves of this miniature succulent have sharp-looking thorns along their edges and as the plant grows they unfold like fierce-looking jaws. The thorns are actually soft, and end in a fragile hair. Tiger-jaws form angular rosettes and produce beautiful yellow or white flowers in late summer.

**Light:** At least four hours of direct sun. **Water:** Allow soil to dry between waterings during growth; water only once or twice in winter. **Temperature:** Normal room temperatures during growth; down to 50°F (10°C) in winter. **Soil:** Standard cactus/succulent mix. **Fertilization:** Feed monthly during growth with high-phosphorus fertilizer. **Propagation:** Divide in spring. **Special Care:** In their native Africa, these succulents grow during our winters and are dormant in our summers, but can adapt to reverse cycle.

**FEROCACTUS** (Devil's-Tongue, Fishhook Cactus)
These cacti are studded with beautiful but vicious spines. Each whorl of thorns contains outer bristlelike gray or white spines and brightly colored central spines, one of which may be curved like a fishhook. Their blue-green bodies are deeply ribbed and grow very slowly into giant globes or columns. The popular devil's-tongue (bottom), *F. latispinus*, is a good houseplant and has red or brown spines.

**Light:** At least six hours of direct sun a day. **Water:** Allow soil to dry somewhat between waterings from spring through fall; water only once or twice in winter. **Temperature:** Normal room temperatures, except in winter when 50°F (10°C) at night is needed. **Soil:** Cactus/succulent mix. **Fertilization:** Feed every two months from spring through fall. **Propagation:** By seed. **Special Care:** Best spine color develops in strong light.

**FICUS** (Rubber Plant, Weeping Fig, Fiddle-Leaf Fig, Banyan Tree, Mistletoe Fig, Creeping Fig, Rusty Fig)

Many species of this diverse genus make excellent houseplants. Some, like the popular rubber plant, grow into large treelike specimens. Others are small and bushy or creeping and trailing. The tree-types are especially durable and adapt well to indoor conditions. The lower-growing kinds are more demanding, needing higher humidity and being more particular about light conditions.

The dark-green-leaved rubber plant, *F. elastica*, is usually the variety 'Decora.' Its large, broad oval leaves have a prominent white midrib and each new leaf is enclosed in a reddish-colored sheath that drops off as the leaf unfolds. The variety 'Doescheri' has dark green leaves that are mottled with gray-green and creamy-yellow. 'Variegata' has leaves with irregular white or creamy-yellow margins and 'Tricolor' has leaves marked with gray-green, yellow and pink.

Rubber trees can grow quite tall and will form well-shaped specimens if they are pruned to encourage branching. The green-leaved kind grows surprisingly well in low light, but the variegated kinds need more light and may be short-lived.

The weeping fig, *F. benjamina*, is an elegant, tall-growing plant with thin branches that bend gracefully downwards at their tips. Its small leaves come to sharp points. *F. benjamina* branches freely without pinching and may grow to the ceiling unless pruned.

The weeping fig is an undemanding plant, but it does appreciate consistency in its environment. The leaves may yellow and drop off if the plant is moved to a new environment with different light, water and humidity conditions. Usually such a shock won't kill the tree and new leaves soon grow to replace those that were lost.

Another foolproof *Ficus* is the fiddle-leaf fig, *F. lyrata*. Its huge leaves are shaped like a fiddle or a violin, with the tips being broader than the bases. These odd-shaped waxy leaves often have wavy edges, which give them even more of an unusual appeal. The rusty fig, *F. rubiginosa*, is a big shrub with bold egg-shaped leaves. Its variety 'Variegata' has leaves marked with creamy-white and green.

Though related to the famous *Ficus* that is grown for its edible figs, most of the houseplant figs do not form fruit indoors. One exception is *F. deltoidea*, the mistletoe fig. This small bushy plant has little round leaves that are dotted with gold and it produces yellow olive-

Pictured on this page: *Ficus benjamina* (top), *F. buxifolia* (middle) and *F. deltoidea* (bottom).

63

like berries throughout the year. Similar in appearance is *F. buxifolia* with small wedge-shaped leaves and delicate red stems.

The thin wiry stems and small heart-shaped leaves of the creeping fig, *F. pumila (F. repens)*, cascade gracefully over the edge of a hanging basket. The plant also grows quite willingly on a support and can even be encouraged to climb up a wall by holding on with its aerial roots. 'Minima' is a variety with extra-small leaves and 'Serphyllifolia' has small lance-shaped leaves. Cream and green mark the leaves of 'Variegata.'

Another trailing species is *F. radicans*. Its leaves are about four inches long and very sharply lance-shaped. Its green and white variegated form is very pretty, but difficult to grow.

The banyan tree, *F. benghalensis*, is a large plant resembling the rubber tree. Its young leaves are covered with fine brown hairs and, when mature, they are marked with yellow-green veins. It produces many gray-barked aerial roots along the main trunk.
**Light:** Tree-types grow best in bright indirect light, but adapt to several hours of direct morning sun and to low indirect light. Variegated-types need more light, but cannot take direct noon sun. Creeping-types cannot tolerate any direct sun. **Water:** For tree-types, allow soil to dry somewhat between waterings. For trailing-types, keep soil moist but not soggy. **Temperature:** Normal room temperatures are fine. Cool winters, not less then 55°F (13°C), are desirable but not necessary. **Soil:** Use standard potting mix. Repot every two years when young, less frequently when mature. *Ficus* species grow well in a slightly root-bound condition. **Fertilization:** Feed with half-strength fertilizer once a month from spring through fall. Do not fertilize during winter. **Propagation:** Tall plants that have lost their lower leaves can be air-layered. After the rooted top is removed, the trunk can be cut back to about five inches and it will resprout new foliage. Stem cuttings may also be taken. On cuttings of large-leaved plants such as a rubber tree, cut each leaf in half to reduce water loss. **Special Care:** Tree-types of *Ficus* need moderate humidity. If the air is too dry, they will be susceptible to red spider mites. Trailing-types need higher humidity and do best if grown on a pebble tray. Wash dust off foliage of large-leaved species. Lower leaves are usually lost with age, but sudden leaf loss is due to overwatering. Dim light or a cold draft will also cause leaf loss. Dry shriveled leaves are due to direct sun.

Pictured on this page: *Ficus elastica* 'Variegata' (top), *F. pumila* (middle) and *F. rubiginosa* 'Variegata' (bottom).

**FITTONIA verschaffeltii** (Mosaic Plant, Nerve Plant)
A creeping plant accustomed to tropical conditions,
the mosaic plant is difficult to grow as a houseplant,
but its striking foliage makes it a plant worth fussing
over. The typical variety has dark green oval leaves
with outstanding rosy-red veins. 'Argyroneura' (top)
displays silver veins and 'Pearcei' has bright carmine
veins and midribs. The dwarf silver-veined variety
'Nana' is much easier to grow since it tolerates lower
humidity.
**Light:** A north window or bright indirect light. **Water:**
Keep soil moist. **Temperature:** Warm room temperatures not below 65°F (18°C). **Soil:** Standard potting
mix with extra peat. **Fertilization:** Feed monthly from
spring through fall. **Propagation:** Take cuttings in
spring. **Special Care:** Grow in a terrarium or on a
pebble tray. Yellow wilting foliage is due to overwatering.

**FUCHSIA** (Fuchsia, Lady's-Eardrops)
Some fuchsias grow as upright bushes, others have
trailing stems, but both kinds produce dazzling flowers with delicate protruding stamens and pistils. Blossoms may be single or double, solid-colored, or bicolored in white and beautiful shades of purple, pink,
red and violet.
    Most fuchsias bloom abundantly from spring into
fall and then go into a dormant period and drop their
leaves. Some hybrids need no rest period and will
bloom throughout the year. They are perfect plants
for hanging baskets on semi-shaded porches or patios
and do well indoors in an east window.
**Light:** Needs four hours of direct sun each day, but
avoid hot noon sun. Morning sun is best. **Water:** Keep
soil moist but not soggy. Uses a great deal of water if
grown outdoors where wind and sun are very drying.
**Temperature:** Cool room temperatures are best. During dormancy, temperature should be about 50°F
(10°C). **Soil:** Standard potting mix with extra soil. **Fertilization:** Feed every two weeks during spring and
summer. Do not feed during dormancy. **Propagation:**
Take stem cuttings from new growth in spring or summer. **Special Care:** Move plant to a cool, bright location in early fall if blooming ceases, and allow soil to
dry somewhat between waterings. A cool basement
or an unheated room is a good location. At the end of
February, bring plant back to warm temperatures, cut
back severely and resume regular watering and fertilizing. Pinch and prune to encourage bushiness.
Whitefly may be a problem.

65

## GARDENIA jasminoides (Gardenia, Cape Jasmine)

A notoriously difficult plant to grow and bloom, gardenia demands consistent care, high humidity, good light and cool night temperatures. If you baby this plant, it will reward you with heavily scented creamy-white blossoms beginning in winter and lasting as long as cool nights prevail.

**Light:** Needs four hours of morning sun. **Water:** Keep soil moist. **Temperature:** Room temperatures during the day, but needs 60° to 65°F (16° to 18°C) at night to set flower buds. **Soil:** Use a mixture of half peat and half potting soil. **Fertilization:** Feed monthly with acid-type fertilizer. **Propagation:** Take cuttings anytime. **Special Care:** Grow on pebble tray and mist frequently. Stem tips turn black and leaves drop if humidity is low. Flower buds will drop from temperature change, under- or overwatering.

## GASTERIA (Gasteria, Ox-Tongue)

The thick flat blunt-ended leaves of the gasteria are dotted with white wartlike areas and are usually arranged in two ranks, giving the stemless plant a fan-shaped appearance. During the summer, orange or red bell-shaped flowers appear on long stalks if the plant is grown in sufficient sun.

**Light:** Four hours of direct sun a day is best, though adapts to north window and bright indirect light. **Water:** Allow soil to dry somewhat between waterings during growth; water only enough to keep plants from shriveling in winter. **Temperature:** Normal room temperatures. **Soil:** Standard cactus/succulent mix. **Fertilization:** Feed once in spring and once in summer with half-strength fertilizer. **Propagation:** Divide or take leaf cuttings in spring. Let cut surface dry before rooting. **Special Care:** Needs low humidity.

## GLORIOSA (Glory Lily)

This unusual vine climbs by grasping onto supports with tendrils that tip the ends of its leaves. The stems grow from a tuber and can reach heights of four to six feet in six months. Large yellow and red blossoms adorn the vine for several months in summer or fall.

**Light:** Bright indirect light or some direct sun. **Water:** Keep soil moist during growth, dry during dormancy. **Temperature:** Warm room temperatures not below 60°F (16°C) during growth; about 50°F (10°C) during rest. **Soil:** Standard potting mix. **Fertilization:** Feed every two weeks in spring and summer. **Propagation:** Divide in spring. **Special Care:** Plant tubers one inch below soil surface in late winter; keep at 68° to 70°F (20° to 21°C) until growth emerges. After flowering, withhold water and let foliage die. Store tuber in pot.

### GREVILLEA robusta (Silk Oak)

The feathery leaves of the silk oak actually have a soft satiny feel because of the very fine hairs that cover their surfaces. A huge sixty-foot tree in its native Australia, when grown indoors the silk oak adds at least a foot of growth each year. When it reaches the ceiling, it's time to start again.

**Light:** Some direct sun from an east or west exposure, but avoid direct noon sun. **Water:** Allow soil to dry somewhat between waterings. **Temperature:** Cool room temperatures. **Soil:** Standard potting mix. **Fertilization:** Feed once a month with quarter-strength fertilizer. **Propagation:** Stem cuttings are difficult to root; seeds sprout easily. **Special Care:** Likes high humidity; grow on a pebble tray. Do not mist foliage directly. Prune to encourage branching.

### GUZMANIA (Guzmania)

Long before the showy flower stalk emerges, the central leaves of a guzmania turn brilliant scarlet as a signal that it is preparing to bloom. *G. lingulata* is an epiphytic species with strap-shaped leaves and pink or red flower bracts. Its variety 'Splendens' has purple-striped foliage. A terrestrial species with golden bracts, *G. musaica* has dark green- and purple-banded leaves. Many other species are grown.

**Light:** Bright indirect light in summer; some direct sun in winter. **Water:** Keep soil moist and vase formed by leaves full of water. **Temperature:** Room temperatures. **Soil:** Orchid/bromeliad mix for epiphytes; standard potting mix with extra peat for terrestrials. **Fertilization:** Feed monthly. **Propagation:** Remove offsets after main plant dies. **Special Care:** Needs high humidity.

### GYMNOCALYCIUM (Chin Cactus, Plaid Cactus, Moon Cactus)

Little knobs beneath the spines on these round cacti resemble chins, thus the common name chin cactus. By far the most popular plants of this genus are the mutant forms of the faintly red-banded plaid cactus, *G. mihanovichii.* Called moon cactus, they lack the green pigment chlorophyll and are colored rosy red, creamy yellow, or purplish black. Without chlorophyll these cacti cannot live on their own, so they are grafted onto green cacti to receive sustenance.

**Light:** At least four hours of direct sun a day. **Water:** Allow soil to dry somewhat in summer; water only once or twice in winter. **Temperature:** Cool room temperatures. **Soil:** Standard cactus/succulent mix. **Fertilization:** Feed once in spring. **Propagation:** Offsets of mutant forms must be grafted onto green cacti. **Special Care:** Needs low humidity.

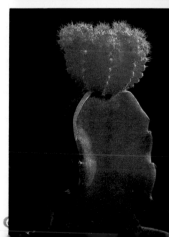

**GYNURA** (Velvet Plant, Purple Passion Vine)
The jagged-edged hairy leaves of these plants have the plush feel and look of velvet. When given sufficient sun, the hairs on the young foliage are an iridescent purple and the plant gleams in the sunlight. *G. aurantiaca*, the velvet plant, is upright growing and *G. sarmentosa* (top), the purple passion vine, is a trailing plant. Both produce orange-yellow dandelionlike blooms in spring that have an unpleasant odor. Pinch off flower buds before they open.
**Light:** Does best in an eastern exposure. **Water:** Keep soil moist. **Temperature:** Normal room temperatures. **Soil:** Standard potting mix. **Fertilization:** Feed monthly from spring through fall. **Propagation:** Take cuttings anytime. **Special Care:** Pinch regularly to keep attractive shape. Young plants have best purple color.

**HAEMANTHUS** (Blood Lily)
These unusual bulbous plants produce tall flowering stalks topped by giant red, pink, or white balls of yellow-tipped stamens. *H. katharinae* and *H. multiflorus* bloom in the spring after a winter dormant period during which the foliage dies back. *H. albiflos* is evergreen, though it too rests in winter. Bulbs for these uncommon houseplants are usually bought and planted in spring.
**Light:** Needs four hours of direct morning sun a day. **Water:** Keep soil moist during growth. Allow deciduous kinds to dry thoroughly during dormancy and evergreen kinds to dry only slightly. **Temperature:** Normal room temperatures during growth; about 55°F (13°C) during rest. **Soil:** Standard potting mix. **Fertilization:** Feed monthly during growth. **Propagation:** Divide bulbs when repotting. **Special Care:** Plant bulbs with tip just above soil.

**HAWORTHIA** (Zebra Haworthia, Fairy-Washboard)
The haworthias are one of the few succulents that don't need direct sun. The gray, brown, or green leaves are usually dotted or striped with warty white growths and are arranged in compact rosettes. *H. fasciata*, the zebra haworthia, has upright leaves with bold white markings on the undersides. *H. attenuata* (bottom) has markings on the undersides as well as a central stripe on the topsides. The fairy-washboard, *H. limifolia*, has horizontal markings on both sides.
**Light:** Curtain-filtered southern or western exposure. **Water:** Allow to dry somewhat between waterings. **Temperature:** Cool room temperatures. **Soil:** Standard cactus/succulent mix. **Fertilization:** Feed once each spring. **Propagation:** Divide in spring or take leaf cuttings. **Special Care:** Rots if overwatered.

## HEBE andersonii (Veronica)

Hybrids of this evergreen plant produce fluffy spikes of flowers in purple, white, red, or violet during late summer and fall. Though frequently grown outdoors as a hedge plant in the Southwest, this veronica is also grown in a tub as a plant for cool indoor situations such as an enclosed porch or an entryway.

**Light:** Four hours of direct sun a day. **Water:** Keep soil moist. **Temperature:** Cool room temperatures during growth, but needs winter temperatures of 45° to 50°F (7° to 10°C) beginning after flowers fade. **Soil:** Standard potting mix. **Fertilization:** Feed once a month from spring through fall. **Propagation:** Take tip cuttings from new growth in spring. **Special Care:** Cut back halfway after flowering. Will drop flowers and leaves if temperature is too warm.

## HEDERA (Ivy)

Two species of ivy are frequently grown as house plants—*H. helix*, English ivy, and *H. canariensis*, Canary Island ivy. English ivy, the ivy commonly grown as an evergreen vine or ground cover outdoors in cold climates, has glossy dark-green sharply-lobed leaves with white veins. Its leaves are smaller than those of the frost-tender Canary Island ivy, whose foliage can measure up to six inches across.

Both species come in green-leaved or variegated forms. *H. canariensis* 'Variegata' (middle) boasts dark- and light-green-mottled foliage with a broad irregular creamy border. 'Marginemaculata' has cream-colored leaf borders which are speckled with green.

*H. helix* offers many varieties, some displaying variegations of cream, white, yellow, pink and shades of green and others with unusual leaf shapes. 'Glacier' (bottom) has cream-bordered leaves. 'Sweetheart' has deep green heart-shaped leaves. The leaves of 'Itsy Bitsy' measure a mere half-inch long. 'Irish Lace' has deeply cut foliage with a lacy appearance.

**Light:** Tolerates low light, but bright indirect light is best; some direct sun is acceptable in winter. Variegated forms need good light. **Water:** Keep soil moist. **Temperature:** Needs cool room temperatures; does best with winter nights about 50° to 55°F (10° to 13°C). Canary Island ivy withstands warmer temperatures; English ivy must be kept cool. **Soil:** Standard potting mix. **Fertilization:** Feed monthly from spring through fall. **Propagation:** Take cuttings from new growth. **Special Care:** Spider mites are a severe problem if air is too dry or temperatures are too warm. Grow in hanging basket or provide support. Variegated or fancy-leaved forms may revert to plain variety; cut out undesirable growth.

69

### HIBISCUS rosa-sinensis (Hibiscus, Rose-of-China)

The large papery flowers of hibiscus last only for a day or two, but if the plant is well grown, new buds open almost every day from spring to autumn. White, pink, yellow, orange and red varieties are available, and a red-flowered variety, 'Cooperi,' offers white-and-green-mottled leaves for a particularly colorful show.

**Light:** Four hours of direct sun a day. **Water:** Keep soil moist. **Temperature:** Normal room temperatures; 55° to 60°F (13° to 16°C) at night during winter. **Soil:** Standard potting mix. **Fertilization:** Feed monthly during growing season. **Propagation:** Take cuttings in late spring. **Special Care:** Cut back stems to several inches in early spring. Flower buds may drop due to dry soil, cold drafts, or underfeeding. Leaves will curl if humidity is too low. Repot every spring.

### HIPPEASTRUM (Amaryllis)

The spectacular trumpet-shaped blossoms of an amaryllis bloom in clusters of two to six flowers atop a one- or two-foot-tall stem. There are many hybrids available in every shade of red, pink, orange and white, and striped and bicolored varieties are common.

**Light:** Needs four hours of direct sun a day; keep out of sun while in bloom. **Water:** Keep soil moist while in growth. **Temperature:** Normal room temperatures. **Soil:** Standard potting mix. **Fertilization:** Feed every two weeks while in growth. **Propagation:** Divide offsets when repotting. **Special Care:** In fall, move plant to dim location and stop watering. In winter, bring back into bright spot and resume watering. If no flowers form, bulb is undernourished; feed and provide more light to encourage flowers the following season.

### HOWEA forsterana (Kentia Palm, Sentry Palm)

This tall vase-shaped palm is one of the best palms you can grow as a houseplant. Sentry palm is a slow-growing plant that is undemanding, tolerating low light and a pot-bound condition. The feathery arching foliage arises from a single trunk, but tubs are often planted with several palms to create the illusion of a full multiple-trunked plant.

**Light:** Does best in bright indirect light, but withstands low light and curtain-filtered sun. **Water:** Keep soil moist during growing season; allow to dry somewhat in winter. **Temperature:** Normal room temperatures. **Soil:** Standard potting mix with some rotted cow manure added. **Fertilization:** Feed monthly with half-strength fertilizer from spring to fall. **Propagation:** Sow fresh seeds. **Special Care:** Cut off brown leaf tips, which result from low humidity.

## HOYA (Wax Plant)

These slow-growing woody-stemmed vines have thick, somewhat succulent leaves with a long oval shape and pointed tips. Large clusters of tiny waxy blooms appear in spring. The sweetly fragrant blossoms are long lasting if the plant is kept cool and out of direct sunlight, and if it is not moved.

The miniature wax plant (top), *H. bella*, offers small pointed leaves and clusters of white flowers with crimson centers. It is a bit reluctant to bloom, needing cool winter temperatures and good light.

More commonly grown, *H. carnosa* (middle) has larger leaves than *H. bella* and its trailing stems are sometimes adorned with variegated foliage. 'Exotica' has green leaves colored with yellow and pink. 'Variegata' is white-margined and 'Krinkle Kurl,' sometimes called the Hindu-rope vine, bears curiously twisted leaves. Flowers of all these varieties are white with red centers and are borne in rounded clusters.

**Light:** Needs four hours of direct sun a day to bloom, but tolerates all kinds of light, even low light. Variegated patterns are best with good light. **Water:** Allow soil to dry somewhat between waterings from spring through fall; allow to dry more in winter. **Temperature:** Normal room temperatures from spring through fall; needs cool winters, about 55°F (13°C), if plant is to bloom. **Soil:** Standard potting mix. **Fertilization:** Feed once in spring and once in summer. **Propagation:** Take stem cuttings during the growing season; plant may be air-layered. **Special Care:** Tie vines to support if climbing plant is desired, otherwise grow in hanging basket. Do not move plant after flower buds are visible. Do not remove faded flowers since new flowers grow from the same stem.

## HYACINTHUS orientalis (Hyacinth)

A pot of hyacinths forced to bloom indoors in winter will fill a room with a heady sweet perfume that is a delightful precursor of spring. The tall stalks of waxy pink, white, lavender, purple, or yellow flowers are long lasting if kept cool. Hyacinth bulbs can be grown suspended above water in a special bulb vase, or planted in a pot of soil.

**Light:** After planting, keep in a dim or dark spot until roots are formed, then move to curtain-filtered light. **Water:** Keep soil moist or bulb suspended one inch above water level. **Temperature:** After planting, keep bulbs below 50°F (10°C) for at least eight weeks, then keep at about 60°F (16°C). **Soil:** Standard potting mix. **Fertilization:** Do not feed. **Propagation:** Done only by experts. **Special Care:** Plant bulbs one inch beneath soil surface in fall. Discard after flowering.

71

## HYDRANGEA macrophylla (Hydrangea, Hortensia)

Laden with enormous balls of flowers, hydrangeas are one of the showiest gift plants sold in spring. They come in white and shades of pink, blue, lavender and purple. Hydrangeas are difficult to rebloom as houseplants, but may be planted outdoors as garden shrubs in areas where winters do not fall below 0°F (-18°C).

**Light:** Bright indirect light while in bloom. Eastern exposure if reblooming. **Water:** Keep soil moist; never let dry out. **Temperature:** Cool room temperatures. **Soil:** Standard potting mix. **Fertilization:** Do not feed blooming plants. Apply acid-type fertilizer monthly in summer to plants being rebloomed. **Propagation:** Take cuttings in midsummer. **Special Care:** To rebloom, cut back plants after flowering; summer outdoors in half-shade until frost, then move indoors to sunny spot about 45°F (7°C) until January.

## HYMENOCALLIS (Peruvian Daffodil, Spider Lily)

The unusual flowers of the Peruvian daffodil have a fringed central cup framed by six long curling petallike sepals. Several white or yellow fragrant blossoms are borne atop the tall flower stalk in midsummer. The bulbs can be kept from year to year.

**Light:** Four hours of direct sun a day. **Water:** Keep moist from February until fall when water should be withheld to cause foliage to die back. **Temperature:** In February, place pot containing dormant bulbs in warm spot, such as over a radiator; when shoots emerge, move to cooler location. Store dormant bulbs at about 60°F (16°C). **Soil:** Standard potting mix. **Fertilization:** Feed every two weeks. **Propagation:** Divide bulbs in fall. **Special Care:** Leave dormant bulbs in pot and do not water or feed until February.

## HYPOCYRTA (Clog Plant, Goldfish Plant)

The small orange or scarlet blossoms of this gesneriad are puffed up into little pouches that end in a tiny opening. Several species are cultivated and most bloom prolifically from spring through summer and rest in winter. The foliage on the arching stems is shiny dark green on top and light green or reddish beneath. These plants are often sold under the names *Nematanthus* or *Alloplectus*.

**Light:** Curtain-filtered light. **Water:** Keep moist from spring through fall; allow to dry somewhat in winter. **Temperature:** Normal room temperatures during growth, cooler in winter. **Soil:** Standard potting mix with some extra peat. **Fertilization:** Feed monthly. **Propagation:** Stem cuttings anytime. **Special Care:** Cut the stems back severely after flowering, since blooms appear on new growth. Needs high humidity.

### HYPOESTES sanguinolenta (Pink Polka-Dot Plant, Freckle-Face)

As its name suggests, the leaves of this cute plant are speckled with pink dots. The varieties 'Pink Brocade' and 'Splash' are even more brightly colored than the common species. A vigorous grower, the pink polka-dot plant must be pinched and pruned regularly to maintain its shape. If it becomes leggy, it's best to renew the plant from cuttings.

**Light:** Curtain-filtered sun creates the best color patterns; bright indirect light is acceptable. **Water:** Keep soil moist. **Temperature:** Normal room temperatures. **Soil:** Standard potting mix with some extra peat. **Fertilization:** Feed monthly with quarter-strength fertilizer. **Propagation:** Take cuttings anytime. **Special Care:** Needs high humidity; grow on pebble tray or mist frequently. Pinch regularly.

### IMPATIENS (Impatiens, Busy Lizzy, Balsam)

Often grown outdoors as annuals, these flowering plants are well suited for indoor culture. Busy Lizzy, *I. wallerana*, grows into a spreading mound covered with flat blossoms that come in a wide range of brilliant colors. Many new hybrids offer foliage variegated with purple, cream and light green. Balsam (middle), *I. balsamina*, is an upright plant with rose-shaped blossoms in an array of pastel hues lining its stems.

**Light:** Curtain-filtered light or bright indirect light. **Water:** Keep soil moist. **Temperature:** Normal room temperatures. **Soil:** Standard potting mix. **Fertilization:** Feed once a month. **Propagation:** Take stem cuttings anytime. **Special Care:** Pinch plants regularly to maintain an attractive shape. If plants become ungainly, renew from cuttings. Keep out of cold drafts.

### IPOMOEA (Morning-Glory)

This twining vine, well loved for its ability to adorn fences and gates with heart-shaped leaves and trumpet-shaped blossoms, is just as pretty when grown indoors. Sow the seed in midsummer and you'll have a window full of foliage and flowers all fall and winter. The vines can be trained to grow on a trellis or on strings suspended from a curtain rod. Large-flowered hybrids are available in lovely shades of blue, lavender, purple and white.

**Light:** At least four hours of direct sun a day. **Water:** Keep soil moist. **Temperature:** Normal room temperatures. **Soil:** Standard potting mix. **Fertilization:** Feed monthly with high-phosphorus fertilizer. **Propagation:** Sow seeds in a large pot in midsummer; thin to four best seedlings. **Special Care:** Provide support. Discard plant after flowering.

73

## IRESINE (Bloodleaf, Chicken-Gizzard)

Like most plants with colorful leaves, bloodleaf produces the richest color when grown in bright light or full sun. The stems and narrow leaves of *I. lindenii* are deep blood-red with rose veins. *I. herbstii* (top) has dark wine-red heart-shaped leaves with pale red veins, and its variety 'Aureo-reticulata' offers red stems and yellow veins on green leaves.

**Light:** Three or more hours of full sun a day. May be grown in southern exposure. **Water:** Keep soil moist. **Temperature:** Normal room temperatures. **Soil:** Standard potting mix. **Fertilization:** Feed every two weeks from spring through fall. **Propagation:** Take cuttings in spring or summer. **Special Care:** Pinch to encourage bushiness. Cut back straggly plants or renew from cuttings. Does best with moderate to high humidity.

## JACARANDA mimosifolia (Jacaranda)

This elegant large plant is seldom grown as a houseplant though it is a popular garden tree in tropical and semitropical areas. The long graceful leaves are finely divided into many lacy leaflets, giving the plant a fernlike appearance. Jacaranda is easy to grow as a houseplant and, though it doesn't produce its beautiful blue flowers indoors, it will grow into a becoming, tall specimen.

**Light:** Several hours of direct sun each day. **Water:** Allow soil to dry somewhat between waterings. **Temperature:** Normal room temperatures. **Soil:** Standard potting mix. **Fertilization:** Feed monthly from spring through fall. **Propagation:** Take stem cuttings from new growth. **Special Care:** Pinch stems regularly. Does best with moderate to high humidity. May lose foliage briefly in spring, but new leaves soon regrow.

## JACOBINIA carnea (Brazilian-Plume, Plume Flower)

In late summer, Brazilian plumes produce fluffy clusters of tubular flowers on the tips of their stems. Colored rose-purple or pink, the blossoms last several weeks and when they fade the plant should be cut back. This plant may be difficult to grow outside of a greenhouse since it requires high humidity and strong light. Brazilian plume is often named *Justicia carnea*.

**Light:** Four hours of direct sun a day in winter and a curtain-filtered southern exposure in summer. **Water:** Keep soil moist. **Temperature:** Normal room temperatures; not below 60°F (16°C) in winter. **Soil:** Standard potting mix. **Fertilization:** Feed monthly from spring through fall. **Propagation:** Take cuttings from new growth in spring. **Special Care:** Cut back severely after flowering or in spring. Provide high humidity.

### JASMINUM (Jasmine, Jessamine)

Richly scented with a sweet perfume, jasmine is a favorite flowering plant among indoor gardeners. Several species are popular and all have the same cultural requirements. *J. officinale* (top) blooms throughout the summer bearing clusters of white flowers on its vining stems. Pink jasmine, *J. polyanthum*, blooms in spring, bearing white star-shaped blossoms that unfold from pink buds.

**Light:** Four hours of direct sun a day; protect from noon sun in summer. **Water:** Keep soil moist. **Temperature:** Normal room temperatures during the day, but must have winter nights of 40° to 50°F (4° to 10°C). **Soil:** Standard potting mix. **Fertilization:** Feed every two weeks from spring to fall. **Propagation:** Take stem cuttings anytime. **Special Care:** Needs high humidity. Cut back severely after flowering. Provide support.

### KALANCHOE blossfeldiana (Kalanchoe)

When the days are short, offering less than twelve hours of light, this succulent produces its brilliant flower clusters. To trick kalanchoes into blooming for the winter holidays, florists darken the greenhouse beginning in August. The species is red-flowered, but many hybrids with huge clusters of red, orange, pink, salmon, or yellow flowers are now available.

**Light:** At least four hours of direct sun a day. **Water:** Allow soil to dry somewhat between waterings. **Temperature:** Normal room temperatures. **Soil:** Standard cactus/succulent mix. **Fertilization:** Feed with low-nitrogen fertilizer every two weeks when in bloom. **Propagation:** Take cuttings in summer. **Special Care:** Difficult to rebloom. For Christmas blossoms, try keeping the plant in a dark closet from 7:00 p.m. until 8:00 a.m. beginning September 1.

### KALANCHOE tomentosa (Panda Plant, Plush Plant)

The oval leaves of this succulent are so densely hairy that they appear to be covered with gray fur! And to add to their curious appeal, the tips of the leaves are marked with reddish-brown spots. Panda plants must have strong light to look their best. In weak light the hairs become sparse and the lower leaves drop.

**Light:** At least six hours of direct sun a day. **Water:** Allow soil to dry somewhat between waterings from spring through fall; allow to dry thoroughly in winter. **Temperature:** Normal room temperatures during growth; down to 50°F (10°C) in winter. **Soil:** Standard cactus/succulent mix. **Fertilization:** Feed once in spring and once in summer. **Propagation:** Take stem or leaf cuttings; allow cut surface to dry before rooting. **Special Care:** Keep out of noon sun in summer.

## KOHLERIA (Kohleria, Tree Gloxinia)

Several species of *Kohleria* are grown for their soft hairy leaves and tubular flowers, but it's the hybrids that put on the best show. Often blooming year-round rather than only in spring and summer, they offer larger flowers in a variety of colors. 'Carnival' has red flowers spotted with yellow. 'Longwood' has red flowers with dark red and white spots, and 'Rongo' has magenta blossoms with dark pink spots.

**Light:** Bright indirect or curtain-filtered light. **Water:** Keep moist. **Temperature:** Warm room temperatures. **Soil:** Standard potting mix with extra peat. **Fertilization:** Feed monthly. **Propagation:** Take stem cuttings in spring. **Special Care:** May become semi-dormant in winter; water less and do not fertilize until growth resumes. Needs moderate to high humidity.

## LAMPRANTHUS (Ice Plant)

When the sun plays off the many-petaled blooms of the ice plant, their satiny gleam is breathtaking. Flower colors include shocking pink, red, yellow, purple and white, and blossoms open only when the sun shines. Many species are grown outdoors as groundcovers in warm climates, but they also make good houseplants. All have thick, succulent leaves and stems, which have a tendency to trail.

**Light:** At least four hours of direct sun a day. **Water:** Allow soil to dry somewhat between waterings from spring through fall; water only enough to keep plant from shriveling in winter. **Temperature:** Normal room temperatures. **Soil:** Standard cactus/succulent mix. **Fertilization:** Feed monthly with low-nitrogen fertilizer during growth. **Propagation:** Take stem cuttings; let cut surface dry before rooting. **Special Care:** Cool winter temperatures encourage flowering in spring.

## LAURUS nobilis (Sweet Bay, Laurel)

The aromatic leaves of sweet bay are used to flavor food, and an oil is extracted from them for use in perfumes and medicines. Though it's a challenge to grow this shrub indoors—it demands very cool conditions and bright light in winter—the rewards of having fresh bay leaves for cooking make it worth a try.

**Light:** Eastern or curtain-filtered southern exposure. **Water:** Keep soil moist. **Temperature:** Normal room temperatures during growth; needs winters of about 45°F (7°C). **Soil:** Standard potting mix with extra peat. **Fertilization:** Feed monthly with acid-type fertilizer in spring and summer. **Propagation:** Stem cuttings are difficult to root; take in fall and use rooting hormone, keeping in a very cool bright place until spring. **Special Care:** May be summered outdoors in bright light.

## LIRIOPE muscari (Big Blue Lilyturf)

Commonly grown as a groundcover outdoors in southern areas, big blue lilyturf is easy to grow as a houseplant, though it is rarely seen. The plant forms a vase-shaped mound of grasslike leaves that are either solid green or green bordered with cream-colored stripes. Delicate spikes of violet, purple, or white flowers rise above the foliage in late summer.

**Light:** Bright indirect or curtain-filtered light. **Water:** Keep soil moist during the growing season; allow to dry between waterings in winter. **Temperature:** Normal room temperatures from spring to fall; as cool as possible during winter. **Soil:** Standard potting mix. **Fertilization:** Feed monthly from spring through summer. **Propagation:** Divide in spring. **Special Care:** Provide some direct sun for variegated forms.

## LITHOPS (Living-Stones, Flowering Stones)

These tiny succulents are charming when planted among pebbles in a shallow dish garden—at first glance they are easily mistaken for stones! Composed of two fat leaves that store water, living stones may produce beautiful white or yellow daisylike blossoms in fall. Then two new leaves emerge from between the old leaves, which slowly shrivel up.

**Light:** At least four hours of direct sun a day. **Water:** Allow soil to dry well between waterings in spring and fall. Do not water in summer and winter or when new leaves are forming, since new growth absorbs water from the old leaves. **Temperature:** Normal room temperatures; 50°F (10°C) is desirable in winter. **Soil:** Standard cactus/succulent mix. **Fertilization:** Do not feed. **Propagation:** Divide clumps. **Special Care:** Needs low humidity. Overwatering will cause rot.

## LOBIVIA (Cob Cactus)

These cacti can be globular or columnar, have widely-spaced or closely-spaced spines and grow as a single stem or in clumps, but they all flower freely in summer, producing enormous many-petaled blossoms. Flowers are red, orange, purple, pink, or yellow and last only a day or two, though new flowers appear frequently throughout the summer.

**Light:** At least four hours of direct sun a day. **Water:** Let soil dry somewhat between waterings from spring through summer; water only once or twice in winter. **Temperature:** Room temperatures during growth; 50°F (10°C) in winter to encourage blooming. **Soil:** Standard cactus/succulent mix. **Fertilization:** Feed monthly in spring and summer with quarter-strength high-phosphorus fertilizer. **Propagation:** Sow seeds or divide clumps. **Special Care:** Low humidity.

77

## LYCASTE (Lycaste, Nun Orchid)

These orchids are easy-to-grow houseplants since they are compact and like cool winter temperatures. Two or three long leaves and a flower stalk bearing a single large fragrant blossom grow from each pseudobulb. *L. cruenta* (top) has beautiful golden blossoms that appear on and off all year. The nun orchid, *L. virginalis*, blooms in winter and has pure white blossoms. Its many varieties offer flowers tinted or spotted with rose, violet, purple, or crimson.

**Light:** East window or curtain-filtered southern exposure. **Water:** Keep moist. **Temperature:** Cool room temperatures, down to 50°F (10°C) at night. **Soil:** Epiphytic orchid mix. **Fertilization:** Feed monthly. **Propagation:** Divide pseudobulbs in spring. **Special Care:** Stop watering for two weeks in fall and allow foliage to wither; resume watering when new growth emerges.

## MAMMILLARIA (Nipple Cactus)

This diverse group of cacti offers compact plants that may grow as simple ball-shaped stems, in clumps, or as rounded or cylindrical plants with knobby branches. Nipple cacti may be very bristly or only slightly bristly, but they are usually recognizable by two characteristics: They have no ribs, but their spines grow from the tips of nipplelike swellings arranged in whorls around the stem; and the small flowers often appear in rings around the top of the plant.

There are hundreds of species of *Mammillaria* and many of them make excellent houseplants. *M. spinosissima* (middle and bottom) has both white- and brown-tipped bristles and its magenta flowers bloom freely in spring, forming a wreath around the top of the plant. *M. camptotricha*, the bird's-nest cactus, is a squat cactus with very long protuberances tipped with only a few needlelike yellow spines. It bears creamy-white blossoms. In contrast, *M. hahniana*, the old-lady cactus, is densely covered with white wool and spines. Small purplish-red flowers ring the plant in summer.

**Light:** Thorny kinds need at least four hours of direct sun a day; sparsely-thorned kinds need to be shielded from direct noon sun in summer. **Water:** Allow soil to dry somewhat from spring through fall; water only once or twice in winter. **Temperature:** Normal room temperatures during growth; down to 50°F (10°C) at night in winter to encourage blooming. **Soil:** Standard cactus/succulent mix. **Fertilization:** Feed with low-nitrogen fertilizer once in spring and once in summer. **Propagation:** Make cuttings or remove offsets; allow cut surface to dry before rooting. **Special Care:** Repot every spring to speed growth.

78

**MARANTA leuconeura** (Prayer Plant, Rabbit's-Tracks)
Not only are prayer plants beautifully patterned, their
foliage also puts on a daily performance by folding up
along the mid-veins at night and unfolding during the
day. The folded leaves resemble praying hands, hence
the name prayer plant.

Prayer plants have somewhat spreading stems that
look graceful when allowed to trail over the edge of a
pot or along the soil surface. Stalks of small purple,
white, or pink flowers may appear in summer on well-
grown plants.

The variety 'Massangeana' boasts leaves whose upper surfaces are deep blackish green marked with a
feathered pattern of silvery-gray down the center and
whose undersides are wine-red. 'Erythroneura' (middle) has bright rose-red veins and chartreuse blotches
along the central vein. Rabbit's-tracks (top), 'Kerchov-
iana', has gray-green leaves with brown and dark
green paired splotches along the central veins sug-
gesting the footprints of a rabbit.
**Light:** Bright indirect light; avoid direct sun. **Water:**
Keep soil moist during growth; allow to dry somewhat
during the winter: **Temperature:** Warm room temperatures; not below 60°F (16°C) in winter. **Soil:** Standard
potting mix with extra peat added. **Fertilization:** Feed
every two weeks from spring through summer with
half-strength fertilizer. **Propagation:** Take stem cuttings with two or three leaves in spring or summer.
**Special Care:** Needs high humidity or plant will be
stunted and leaf tips will turn brown. Curled and
spotted leaves and yellow lower leaves are due to dry
soil. Withhold food and allow soil to dry slightly in
winter; foliage may die back but new growth emerges
from soil.

**MEDINILLA magnifica** (Medinilla)
This unusual plant with its bizarre flowers and huge
leathery leaves is happiest when grown in a greenhouse, where the humidity can be kept constantly
high. With steadfast attention, however, it can succeed as a houseplant. In spring or summer, large pendulous clusters of shocking pink bracts and flowers
appear and are long lasting.
**Light:** Bright indirect light; avoid direct sun. **Water:**
Keep soil moist during growing season; water sparingly from November through January. **Temperature:**
Warm room temperatures not below 65°F (18°C) during growth. Keep at 60°F (16°C) during rest. **Soil:** Use
epiphytic orchid mix. **Fertilization:** Feed every two
weeks with half-strength fertilizer. **Propagation:** Take
cuttings in spring; provide bottom heat. **Special Care:**
Grow on pebble tray and syringe leaves daily.

79

## MICROCOELUM (Coconut Palm)

This graceful palm, which is grown in the tropics around the world for its economically important coconuts, can be grown as a houseplant too. It won't produce fruit indoors, but will make an ornamental addition to any indoor planting. The dwarf variety, which slowly grows to eight feet tall and has a rough brown trunk, is best suited to indoor culture. Coconut palm is sometimes listed as *Cocos*.

**Light:** Bright indirect or curtain-filtered light. **Water:** Keep soil moist. **Temperature:** Warm room temperatures are best but tolerates cool nights in winter. **Soil:** Standard potting mix. **Fertilization:** Feed once in spring and once in summer. **Propagation:** May be grown from a store-bought coconut planted in soil and kept warm. **Special Care:** Yellow leaves are due to dry soil; brown leaf tips are due to low humidity.

## MICROLEPIA strigosa (Microlepia)

This lush fern is a vigorous grower, producing large bright green fronds even in low light. The delicately divided leaves can grow to three feet long, though the dwarf variety, sometimes named *M. speluncae*, remains more compact with its leaves growing only to one foot long.

**Light:** Does best in bright indirect light, though will grow in low interior light, a north window and in curtain-filtered light. **Water:** Allow soil to dry slightly between waterings. **Temperature:** Normal room temperatures. **Soil:** Standard potting mix with extra peat added. **Fertilization:** Feed monthly in spring and summer. **Propagation:** Divide plant in spring. **Special Care:** Needs high humidity; grow on a pebble tray or in a humidified room. Plant is sensitive to improper watering; do not let soil dry too much.

## MIKANIA ternata (Mikania)

This uncommon plant makes a pretty specimen for a hanging basket or for a position on a table where its trailing stems can cascade freely. The woody stems bear short purplish hairs and small leaves that are divided into five to seven lobes. Gray-green on top, the leaves are purple beneath and young foliage is covered with dense violet hairs that glint in the sun.

**Light:** Curtain-filtered light or some direct sun. **Water:** Allow soil to dry somewhat between waterings. **Temperature:** Normal room temperatures. **Soil:** Standard potting mix. **Fertilization:** Fertilize once a month from spring through summer. **Propagation:** Take cuttings in spring or summer. **Special Care:** May suffer in winter if humidity is too low. Renew from cuttings if plant becomes straggly.

**MONSTERA deliciosa** (Swiss-Cheese Plant, Split-Leaf Philodendron)

All but the young leaves of this climbing jungle plant are slashed and perforated with holes. The deep cuts along the margins develop as the giant foliage matures only if the plant has sufficient light. Long gray aerial roots grow from the stem and should be pushed into the soil in the pot or into a moss-covered stake. A variegated form (top) is commonly grown.

**Light:** Bright indirect light is best; tolerates interior light. **Water:** Allow soil to dry somewhat between waterings. **Temperature:** Normal room temperatures. Tolerates cold winters but may stop growing. **Soil:** Standard potting mix. **Fertilization:** Feed once in spring and once in summer. **Propagation:** Air-layer or take cuttings. **Special Care:** Provide upright support for stems. Leggy growth is due to low light.

**MUSA acuminata** (Dwarf Banana)

Even the dwarf banana is a big plant—it grows to at least six feet tall in a single season and its huge paddle-shaped leaves are four feet long. It bears striking flowers and edible fruits when grown in a greenhouse, but is unlikely to do so as a houseplant. 'Dwarf Cavendish' and 'Sucrier,' which have burgundy markings on the leaves, are popular ornamental varieties.

**Light:** Curtain-filtered southern exposure in summer; direct sun in winter. **Water:** Keep soil moist. **Temperature:** Very warm temperatures during growth; down to 60°F (16°C) in winter. **Soil:** Standard potting mix with extra loam. **Fertilization:** Feed once a month. **Propagation:** Divide by separating shoots that form at base of old stalk. **Special Care:** Plant rests in winter. Main stalk lives one year but new stalks form.

**NARCISSUS** (Paper-White Narcissus, Daffodil)

The paper-white narcissus (bottom) is a delightful bulb to force into bloom for winter enjoyment. The delicate white blossoms are sweetly fragrant and last several weeks if kept cool. Trumpet-flowered daffodils can also be forced for indoor bloom. Buy specially cold-treated bulbs or treat them yourself.

**Light:** Bright indirect light or curtain-filtered sun. **Water:** Keep soil moist. For bulbs grown in pebbles and water, keep water level just beneath bulbs. **Temperature:** Cool room temperatures. **Soil:** Standard potting mix or pebbles and water. **Fertilization:** Not necessary. **Propagation:** Forced bulbs are not increased. **Special Care:** Plant bulbs in late summer or fall. Untreated bulbs need at least eight weeks of dark at 45°F (7°C). (This may be done in refrigerator.) Then give light and warmth. Discard bulbs after blooming.

## NEOPORTERIA (Neoporteria)

These small cacti are native to South America where they grow high in the Andes Mountains. Clusters of colorful spines spring from the tips of lopsided swellings that make up the many ribs. *N. strausiana* (top) has long reddish spines and pink or salmon flowers. *N. chilensis* has white or yellow spines and pale pink flowers. *N. napina* has jet black spines and yellowish blossoms. All bloom in fall.

**Light:** Curtain-filtered southern exposure. **Water:** Allow soil to dry somewhat from spring through fall. Water only once or twice in winter. **Temperature:** Cool room temperatures down to 40° to 45°F (4° to 7°C) at night in winter. **Soil:** Standard cactus/succulent mix. **Fertilization:** Feed once in spring and once in summer with half-strength low-nitrogen fertilizer. **Propagation:** Sow seeds. **Special Care:** Needs low humidity.

## NEOREGELIA (Fingernail Plant)

These striking bromeliads grow as spreading rosettes of highly polished leaves. When a plant is ready to flower, the inner foliage changes color, though the flower stalk never rises out of the central vase. *N. carolinae* (top) is bright green with scarlet central leaves. 'Meyendorffii' is a miniature version; 'Tricolor' has leaves variegated with white, pink and green. *N. spectabilis* has gray-striped leaves with red tips.

**Light:** Bright indirect light from spring through fall; curtain-filtered in winter. **Water:** Keep soil slightly moist and vase filled with water. **Temperature:** Normal room temperatures. **Soil:** Epiphytic bromeliad mix. **Fertilization:** Feed monthly with quarter-strength fertilizer applied to moist soil. **Propagation:** Remove pups from base of mother plant. **Special Care:** Needs high humidity. Plant dies about a year after flowering.

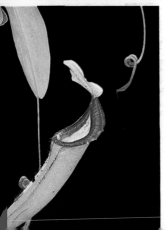

## NEPENTHES (Pitcher Plant)

These tropical insectivorous plants grow suspended from treetops or creep along the jungle floor, luring insects into their hollow "pitchers" where they are trapped and then digested to provide nutrients. Every leaf sprouts a tendril from its tip that later grows into a curious curved pitcher. The pitchers may be speckled or blotched with red or purple. The many species and hybrids all need a warm humid greenhouse.

**Light:** Bright indirect light. **Water:** Keep soil moist. **Temperature:** Warm temperatures, not below 65°F (18°C) at night. **Soil:** Grow in a mixture of osmunda fiber and sphagnum. **Fertilization:** Feed once a month with quarter-strength low-nitrogen fertilizer. **Propagation:** Root stem cuttings in sphagnum. **Special Care:** Needs high humidity; syringe leaves daily.

**NEPHROLEPIS exaltata** (Sword Fern, Boston Fern)

The once popular sword fern has been replaced as a common houseplant by its variety 'Bostoniensis,' the Boston fern. Both have emerald-green leaves shaped like giant feathers, though the Boston fern has more graceful arching fronds. 'Compacta,' the dwarf Boston fern, grows only about two feet tall, while the Boston fern can reach five feet. 'Rooseveltii' (top) and 'Fluffy Ruffles' have ruffled or lacy foliage.

**Light:** Bright indirect light, curtain-filtered eastern exposure, or a north window. **Water:** Allow to dry slightly. **Temperature:** Normal room temperatures. Winter nights to 50°F (10°C) are desirable. **Soil:** Standard potting mix. **Fertilization:** Feed every two weeks. **Propagation:** Divide in spring, or secure runner tips to soil where they will sprout new plants. **Special Care:** Grow on pebble tray.

**NERIUM oleander** (Oleander)

Bouquets of pink, red, or white flowers, which are sometimes fragrant, tip the stems of oleanders from June to October. The long leaves are gray-green and arranged in whorls around the stem. This tall bushy plant needs very bright light and a very cool place in winter. It's difficult to grow as a houseplant, being more suited to a greenhouse.

**Light:** Full sun. **Water:** Keep soil moist from spring through fall; water sparingly in winter. **Temperature:** Warm room temperatures during growth; 45°F (7°C) in winter. **Soil:** Standard potting mix. **Fertilization:** Feed monthly during growth. **Propagation:** Take cuttings in summer. **Special Care:** Cut back stems in fall. Keep in an unheated room in winter and outdoors in summer. Plant parts are poisonous if eaten.

**NERTERA granadensis** (Bead Plant)

The creeping stems of this tiny plant produce a dense mat of dainty leaves less than a quarter of an inch across and in spring, minute green flowers hide beneath them. In summer, the whole plant is covered with orange-red berries that are as translucent and shiny as glass beads. Bead plants are short-lived, but can be kept and rebloomed for several years.

**Light:** Bright indirect light with several hours of direct morning sun. **Water:** Keep moist from spring through summer; allow soil to dry somewhat in winter. **Temperature:** Room temperatures from spring through fall; down to 50° to 55°F (10° to 13°C) at night in winter. **Soil:** Standard potting mix. **Fertilization:** Feed monthly with low-nitrogen fertilizer from midsummer until fall. **Propagation:** Take cuttings after berries drop. **Special Care:** Water from beneath.

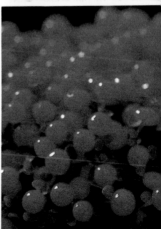

83

**NOTOCACTUS** (Golden Ball, Sun Cup, Silver Ball)
Cacti in this genus have as many as forty ribs and produce big flowers on long stalks. The golden ball (top), *N. leninghausii*, is covered with long yellow bristles, giving the plant a golden glow. *N. apricus*, the sun cup, is named for its three-inch-long yellow blossoms. It has needle-shaped yellow spines. A dense covering of long white bristles pierced by stout brown thorns characterizes *N. scopa*, the silver ball.
**Light:** At least four hours of direct sun. **Water:** Allow soil to dry somewhat between waterings from spring through fall. Water only once or twice in winter. **Temperature:** Normal room temperatures, except in winter when 55°F (13°C) is needed. **Soil:** Standard cactus/succulent mix. **Fertilization:** Feed once in spring and once in summer with low-nitrogen fertilizer. **Propagation:** Remove offsets. **Special Care:** Low humidity.

**ODONTOGLOSSUM** (Tiger Orchid, Lily-of-the-Valley Orchid)
Most species of this genus are best grown in a greenhouse but several do well as houseplants. The blossoms of the tiger orchid (middle), *O. grande*, are gold with cinnamon-brown bands and a speckled shell-shaped lip. Blooms appear in fall or winter and last for months. The easy-to-grow lily-of-the-valley orchid, *O. pulchellum*, has fragrant white flowers with a red-speckled yellow lip. It blooms in autumn.
**Light:** Direct sun from an eastern exposure. **Water:** Keep moist. **Temperature:** Warm days and cool nights down to 50°F (10°C). **Soil:** Osmunda fiber. **Fertilization:** Feed monthly. **Propagation:** Divide pseudobulbs in spring. **Special Care:** Needs high humidity. For one month following blooming, water sparingly but do not allow pseudobulbs to shrivel.

**OLEA europaea** (Olive)
Though it seldom produces its edible black fruits when grown as a houseplant, the olive tree does make an attractive specimen. It can be allowed to grow ceiling-high or be kept pruned into a tidy shrub. The long oblong leaves have a two-toned effect, with dark green topsides and silvery-gray undersides. Tiny highly fragrant flowers are likely to bloom in spring, but since they are not pollinated indoors, olives do not develop.
**Light:** At least four hours of direct sun. **Water:** Let soil dry somewhat between waterings. **Temperature:** Room temperatures. **Soil:** Standard potting mix. **Fertilization:** Feed once in spring and once in summer. **Propagation:** Take cuttings anytime; use rooting hormone and keep in warm place. **Special Care:** Pinch to promote branching. Prune severely in spring if desired.

## OPHIOPOGON (Lilyturf)

These grassy-leaved plants spread rapidly and with annual repotting will easily fill a tub with tall clumps of slender foliage. Dainty stalks of white or pale lavender flowers appear in summer and are followed by blue berries. *O. jaburan* (top) has two-foot-long leaves and comes in several variegated forms. *O. japonicus* has shorter, narrower leaves.

**Light:** Bright indirect light or interior light. **Water:** Keep soil moist. **Temperature:** Normal room temperatures except in winter when should be kept at 40° to 50°F (4° to 10°C). **Soil:** Standard potting mix with extra peat. **Fertilization:** Feed monthly from spring through fall with half-strength fertilizer. **Propagation:** Divide in spring. **Special Care:** Repot into a larger pot each spring.

## OPLISMENUS hirtellus (Basket Grass)

The sparse beauty of the basket grass makes it a perfect plant for giving an Oriental flare to a decorating scheme. Long pointed leaves with faint purple bands are scattered along the slender trailing stems, giving the grass an open airy look. 'Variegatus' has leaves boldly banded with white and tinged with pink, and is often sold under the name *Panicum variegatum*.

**Light:** Bright indirect light with a few hours of direct sun a day; variegated form needs four hours of direct sun. **Water:** Keep soil moist. **Temperature:** Normal room temperatures. Will tolerate coolness or warmth in winter. **Soil:** Standard potting mix. **Fertilization:** Feed monthly from spring through fall with quarter-strength fertilizer. **Propagation:** Take cuttings anytime. **Special Care:** Uses a lot of water in summer. Shade from noon sun.

## OPUNTIA (Prickly Pear, Bunny-Ears, Beaver-Tail)

Instead of having globular stems like most cacti, prickly pears form pads—flattened jointed stems lacking ribs. Two species of this large genus are popular houseplants. Bunny-ears (bottom), *O. microdasys*, has clusters of minute white or yellow thorns that can stick in the skin like slivers of glass. *O. basilaris* has purplish-gray pads and tiny reddish-brown thorns.

**Light:** At least four hours of direct sun a day. **Water:** Let soil dry somewhat between waterings during growth; in winter, water only enough to prevent shriveling. **Temperature:** Room temperatures; 40° to 45°F (4° to 7°C) at night in winter. **Soil:** Cactus/succulent mix. **Fertilization:** Apply low-nitrogen fertilizer once in spring and once in summer. **Propagation:** Use pads as cuttings. **Special Care:** Plants become leggy in insufficient light.

## OREOPANAX capitatus (Oreopanax)

This fast-growing tropical plant is quite tolerant of warm winter temperatures and makes an excellent indoor tree where the thermostat is kept high. The dark green leaves are about five inches long and are borne on equally long stems. This durable plant can grow ceiling-high, but if desired, it can be kept smaller with regular pruning.

**Light:** Several hours of direct morning sun. **Water:** Keep soil moist. **Temperature:** Normal room temperatures are fine. **Soil:** Standard potting mix. **Fertilization:** Feed once a month in spring and summer. **Propagation:** Take stem cuttings and use rooting hormone. **Special Care:** Needs moderate humidity. Wipe dust from foliage. Pinch and prune while young to encourage well-branched plant.

## OXALIS (Wood Sorrel, Lucky Clover, Shamrock Plant)

The foliage of these plants looks like huge clover leaves and the blossoms resemble yellow, white, pink, red, or purple buttercups. Both flowers and leaves fold up at night and open up in the light. *O. megalorrhiza* (middle) has shiny three-lobed leaves and yellow blooms. *O. deppei* bears four-lobed leaves and red or white flowers. Other species and hybrids are also popular.

**Light:** At least four hours of direct sun a day. **Water:** Keep soil moist. **Temperature:** Needs 50° to 60°F (10° to 16°C) at night. **Soil:** Standard potting mix. **Fertilization:** Feed monthly during growth. **Propagation:** Separate offset bulbs. **Special Care:** In fall, plant bulbs one inch deep, several to a pot. When foliage begins to yellow in spring, withhold water and let plant die back. Keep in pot over summer; repot in fall.

## PACYPODIUM lameri (Club-Foot)

This strange plant has a tall cactuslike body covered with thick pink spines and is topped by a whorl of long dark green leaves. The leaves flourish during the growing season and drop off during the dry season. This cycle must be mimicked indoors for this succulent to do well. Plant parts are poisonous if eaten.

**Light:** At least four hours of direct sun a day. **Water:** Allow soil to dry somewhat during growing season; do not water during rest. **Temperature:** Normal room temperatures; down to 55°F (13°C) in winter. **Soil:** Standard potting mix. **Fertilization:** Feed monthly with low-nitrogen fertilizer when in leaf. **Propagation:** Sow seeds that follow flowers. **Special Care:** Plant in a deep pot. Stop watering for several months when leaves start to yellow.

## PACHYSTACHYS lutea (Lollipop Plant)

Beautiful spires of golden-yellow bracts top the stems of the lollipop plant from spring through summer. The tiny white flowers bloom successively from top to bottom, each lasting only a few days. Difficult to grow outside a greenhouse, this plant needs high humidity and good light to rebloom.

**Light:** Bright indirect light with some direct sun in winter; no direct sun in summer. **Water:** Keep moist during growth; allow to dry slightly between waterings during winter. **Temperature:** Normal room temperatures; down to 55°F (13°C) in winter. **Soil:** Standard potting mix. **Fertilization:** Feed every two weeks with high-phosphorus fertilizer from spring to fall. **Propagation:** Take cuttings in spring or summer. **Special Care:** Cut back severely in spring. Provide high humidity. Leaf drop is due to dry soil.

## PANDANUS veitchii (Screw Pine)

The sharp-toothed leaves of this tropical plant are arranged corkscrew fashion around the trunk and leave behind scars when they drop off. Screw pine eventually grows about three feet tall with a tuft of foliage on top and long aerial roots growing from the stem. The leaves of the species have narrow cream or yellow margins and are about two feet long. 'Compacta' has shorter leaves with white margins.

**Light:** Bright indirect light; several hours of direct sun in winter. **Water:** Keep moist during growth; allow soil to dry between waterings in winter. **Temperature:** Keep above 60°F (16°C) in winter. **Soil:** Standard potting mix. **Fertilization:** Feed monthly from spring through fall. **Propagation:** Treat suckers as cuttings. **Special Care:** Needs moderate to high humidity. Plants will die if kept cold and wet.

## PAPHIOPEDILUM (Lady's-Slipper)

Lady's-slippers are the easiest orchids to grow as houseplants. They are compact and form neat clusters of foliage. The exotic-looking blooms have a pouch-shaped petal resembling the toe of a slipper and are beautifully spotted and striped in many stunning color combinations. Green-leaved kinds flower in winter and mottled-leaved kinds flower in summer.

**Light:** Bright indirect light. **Water:** Keep soil moist. **Temperature:** Green-leaved kinds need 50° to 55°F (10° to 13°C) nights and about 70°F (21°C) days; mottled-leaved kinds need 60° to 65°F (16° to 18°C) nights and 70° to 85°F (21° to 29°C) days. **Soil:** Use osmunda fiber. **Fertilization:** Feed monthly with half-strength fertilizer. **Propagation:** Divide in spring. **Special Care:** Keep green-leaved kinds cool during the summer.

## PARODIA (Tom-Thumb Cactus)

These cacti make delightful additions to dish gardens since they grow slowly, remain small and spherical, and bloom freely even while young. Red, orange, or yellow blossoms appear in clusters at the tops of the plants from spring through summer. Spines are often white and the central one may be long and hooked or barbed at the end.

**Light:** At least four hours of direct sun a day. **Water:** Allow soil to dry somewhat between waterings during growth; water only once or twice in winter. **Temperature:** Normal room temperatures during growth; about 50°F (10°C) in winter. **Soil:** Standard cactus/succulent mix. **Fertilization:** Feed once in spring with low-nitrogen fertilizer. **Propagation:** Sow seeds that follow blossoms. **Special Care:** Very sensitive to overwatering in winter; keep dry and cold.

## PASSIFLORA (Passionflower)

The bizarre flowers of this tropical vine have ten petals decorated with a fringe of filaments surrounding prominent pistils and stamens. Blooms last only one day, but appear frequently from July through September. These rampant-growing vines cling with tendrils and should be trained to a trellis. *P. caerula* (middle) has white flowers with a purple fringe. *C. manicata* has scarlet flowers and *P. trifasciata* has pale green blooms tinged with pink and white.

**Light:** At least four hours of direct sun or a southern exposure. **Water:** Keep soil moist. **Temperature:** Room temperatures during growth; about 50°F (10°C) in winter. **Soil:** Standard potting mix. **Fertilization:** Feed monthly while growing. **Propagation:** Take cuttings in spring. **Special Care:** Cut back in spring.

## PEDILANTHUS titymaloides (Devil's-Backbone)

The stems of this peculiar succulent bend sharply at each leaf, creating a zigzag pattern. The variegated-leaved varieties—with green and white foliage, or a green, white and pink combination—are the most popular. Tiny scarlet flowers shaped like birds may tip the branches in summer.

**Light:** Bright indirect light or curtain-filtered light. **Water:** Allow soil to dry somewhat between waterings. **Temperature:** Warm room temperatures; as cool as 50°F (10°C) at night in winter. **Soil:** Standard potting mix. **Fertilization:** Feed once in spring and once in summer with low-nitrogen fertilizer. **Propagation:** Take stem cuttings; allow cut surface to dry before rooting. Sap from stems is a skin irritant. **Special Care:** Needs more moisture and humidity than most succulents. Will drop leaves if plant is too dry.

**PELARGONIUM** (Geranium, Martha Washington Geranium, Ivy Geranium, Scented Geranium)

Geraniums have been popular windowsill plants since grandmother's time. *P. hortorum* (middle) is well known for its beautiful balls of flowers that are held above the foliage on tall stems. Its leaves are scalloped along the edges and are usually marked with a reddish-brown horseshoe-shaped zone.

These old-fashioned favorites come in modern hybrids offering big beautiful clusters of white, red, orange, pink, salmon, or violet flowers. Flower clusters appear profusely in spring and summer and during other seasons if given enough light, warmth and water.

Martha Washington geraniums (top), *P. domesticum*, are stunning plants with crinkled, fan-shaped leaves and clusters of pansylike flowers in shades of pink, purple and white, and are marked with a contrasting blotch. Unlike other geraniums, these need a cool winter rest period or they won't flower.

Lovely in a hanging basket, *P. peltatum*, the ivy geranium, has slender trailing stems and smooth three-pointed leaves. Clusters of narrow-petaled pink, red, white, violet, or bicolored blossoms bloom freely all summer. Ivy geraniums can become quite large and must be pruned regularly.

Scented geraniums are fascinating plants. Many kinds can be collected and all have beautiful foliage, heavily perfumed in familiar fragrances. The scent is released from oil glands on the leaves and is most noticeable when the foliage is gently rubbed or crushed. Rose geranium (bottom), *P. graveolens*, has deeply cut foliage that is rose-scented. Another geranium is *P. tomentosum*, whose velvety leaves are perfumed like peppermint. *P. crispum* has tiny crinkled lemon-scented leaves and yellow variegations.

**Light:** Direct sun from a southern exposure for best bloom. **Water:** Keep soil moist but not soggy. Allow to dry somewhat in winter if keeping cold. **Temperature:** Normal room temperatures. Not below 60°F (16°C) in winter for active growth. Will stop growing but will not be harmed in colder temperatures. Martha Washington geraniums need several months in winter at 45° to 50°F (7° to 10°C) to promote spring and summer flowering. **Soil:** Standard potting mix. **Fertilization:** Feed every two weeks from spring through fall. **Propagation:** Take cuttings from young green stems in spring and summer. **Special Care:** Overwatering will cause rot. Underwatering will slow growth and discourage blooming. Crisp yellow leaves are due to lack of water. Limp yellow leaves are due to too much water. Pinch regularly to keep attractive shape.

### PELLAEA rotundifolia (Button Fern)

This cute little fern flourishes where most other ferns would languish. It can go for days without water and can tolerate even a dry atmosphere. The round, button-shaped leaflets are dark green and are borne along hairy brown stems that arch gently. Button ferns look pretty in low clay pots or in hanging baskets.

**Light:** Bright indirect light from spring through fall; an eastern or western exposure in winter. **Water:** Allow soil to dry somewhat between waterings. **Temperature:** Normal room temperatures during growth; down to 55°F (13°C) in winter. **Soil:** Standard potting mix. **Fertilization:** Feed monthly from spring through fall. **Propagation:** Start from spores, or divide plants in spring. **Special Care:** Trim yellow fronds at soil level.

### PELLIONIA (Trailing Watermelon Begonia, Rainbow Vine)

This dainty creeper isn't a begonia at all, but is so named because its beautiful foliage has the colorful patterns and rosy undersides of many foliage begonias. *P. daveauana* (middle) has stems that can grow to two feet long. Its leaves are bronzy-green with pale central stripes and pink undersides. *P. pulchra*, sometimes called the rainbow vine, has bronzy-green leaves with black veins and purple stems.

**Light:** Bright indirect light. **Water:** Keep soil moist. **Temperature:** Warm room temperatures or 55°F (13°C) in winter. **Soil:** Standard potting mix with extra peat. **Fertilization:** Feed monthly from spring through fall. **Propagation:** Take stem cuttings. **Special Care:** Must have high humidity. Does best in a greenhouse.

### PEPEROMIA (Peperomia)

These wonderful little foliage plants are among the easiest houseplants you can grow, but this doesn't make them any less attractive. There are many species and varieties to choose from and most are semi-succulent plants with thick leathery leaves and a waxy sheen; a few are covered with a soft fine fuzz. Peperomias are undemanding and remain compact, making perfect tabletop plants for decorating a living room or bedroom.

The peperomias fall in three different groups. There are the bushy kinds whose leaves all grow from a central crown. The upright kinds have thick main stems and branches and can grow about a foot tall. The trailing kinds with vining stems are best displayed in hanging containers.

The emerald-ripple peperomia (bottom), *P. caperata*,

is an intriguing plant with deeply puckered leaves displayed on long red petioles. Slender upright flower stalks that resemble white mouse-tails appear in spring. Its variety 'Variegata' has a broad creamy-white border. Another popular bushy type is *P. gris-eoargentea* (middle) with silvery-green wrinkled leaves that are darker along the veins. The watermelon peromia, *P. argyreia*, is a real eye-catcher. The dark green oval leaves have broad bands of silver, similar to the stripes on the rind of a watermelon. The leaf stems are red and the undersides are pink, making the watermelon peperomia an unusual-looking plant.

*P. obtusifolia* (top) is the most well-known peperomia. The round leaves are typically a highly polished emerald-green, but the popular variegated form is a colorful plant with gray-green leaves bordered irregularly with creamy-yellow. Both have supple stems that reach about a foot tall before the weight of the foliage bends them gracefully downwards. The variegated form needs bright light.

The slender, angled stems of *P. puteolata* (bottom) are tinged purplish-red and are studded with whorls of leaves arranged in threes. The foliage has prominent white veins, giving it a striped effect, and pale undersides. Perfect for a hanging basket, this peperomia has trailing stems that are upright at first. It grows full and leafy if kept pinched and pruned. *P. prostrata* is a miniature hanging plant. Its tiny round leaves are marked with silver along the veins and the stems are a pretty red color.

**Light:** Bright indirect light is best; curtain-filtered eastern or western exposure, or low interior light are acceptable. **Water:** Allow soil to dry somewhat between waterings but do not allow plants to wilt. **Temperature:** Normal room temperatures; nights of 55° to 65°F (13° to 18°C) in winter. **Soil:** Standard potting mix. **Fertilization:** Feed once in spring and once in summer. **Propagation:** Take stem cuttings from upright and trailing kinds; take leaf cuttings containing leafstalks from bushy types. **Special Care:** Very sensitive to incorrect watering. Sudden loss of leaves is due to underwatering or cold. Wilted, discolored, or spotted leaves are due to overwatering. Plants will be weak if light is too low. Stems will rot if plants are kept cold and wet in winter. Sudden loss of leaves in winter is due to a cold draft. Keep in small pots; repot only when absolutely necessary.

### PERILEPTA dyeranus (Persian-Shield)

The Persian shield provides a beautiful contrast to green-leaved foliage plants. The iridescent leaves are silvery-purple on top and deep purple beneath. If kept pruned, the plant will grow full and bushy. It will also produce lots of new foliage, which has the best purple color. This is a tricky plant to grow, since it needs warm temperatures and high humidity. Persian shield is sometimes named *Strobilanthes dyeranus*.

**Light:** Bright indirect light. Keep out of direct sun. **Water:** Keep soil moist. **Temperature:** Warm room temperatures. **Soil:** Standard potting mix. **Fertilization:** Feed once a month. **Propagation:** Take cuttings anytime; provide warmth. **Special Care:** Needs high humidity; grow on a pebble tray or in a humidified room.

### PERSEA americana (Avocado)

Watching an avocado plant grow from the large fat seed found inside an avocado pear is fascinating. The seed splits in two and a shoot emerges from the top, seeming to add inches every day. It may take repeated pinching and even severe pruning to encourage the main stem to branch. Avocado plants grow very rapidly into large-leaved treelike specimens.

**Light:** Curtain-filtered southern exposure or morning sun. **Water:** Keep soil moist. **Temperature:** Normal room temperatures; 50°F (10°C) at night in winter is best. **Soil:** Standard potting mix with extra loam. **Fertilization:** Feed monthly from spring through fall. **Propagation:** Start seed in soil; cover, fat end down, in moist soil and keep warm until shoot emerges. **Special Care:** Does best with moderate to high humidity.

### PHILODENDRON (Philodendron)

Philodendrons have been used to decorate homes since Victorian times. Though they prefer moderate to high humidity and warm temperatures, these leafy plants are generally undemanding and flourish in the home with very little attention. Of the hundreds of species native to tropical South American forests, many make excellent indoor plants. Philodendrons fall into two general types: the vining kinds and the upright bushy kinds.

Since they naturally grow from the rain forest floor, twisting and climbing their way up the trunks of tall trees towards the light, the vining types do best if trained to a support. A wooden stake covered with sphagnum moss or bark provides a place for the aerial roots to anchor. When given a place to climb, most vining philodendron species produce very large foliage and thick sturdy stems.

The vining types can also be grown in hanging containers where the stems will cascade to great lengths, or they can be situated where the stems can trail along a tabletop or mantlepiece. But whenever the stems are not allowed to climb, the foliage is smaller and the stems are more slender than they would be if the plant were climbing.

The sweetheart or heart-leaf philodendron (middle), *P. scandens*, is the most well-known vining philodendron. It is an indestructable plant, tolerating low light and all kinds of neglect. It will even grow in plain tap water for years without any added fertilizer. *P. pedatum* (top) has large-lobed leaves and can climb to six or more feet. *P. melanochryson* has huge slightly heart-shaped leaves that are colored black-green with lighter veins. Huge arrow-shaped leaves with burgundy undersides and red leaf stems make *P. erubescens*, the red-leaf philodendron, a very choice climbing plant.

Bushy types produce enormous spreading leaves, but only short trunks—if they produce trunks at all. *P. ilsemannii* (bottom, left) has giant heart-shaped leaves blotched irregularly with ivory, pale and dark green. Growing upright to about five feet, *P. selloum* (bottom) has shallowly lobed leaves with undulating edges. Many varieties of this philodendron are offered; some are dwarf, others are more deeply lobed.

**Light:** Bright indirect light or a curtain-filtered eastern or western exposure is best; *P. scandens* does well also in low light. **Water:** Keep soil moist in growing season; allow soil to dry slightly in winter. **Temperature:** Philodendrons like warmth. Normal room temperatures are fine; will tolerate winter temperatures down to 50°F (10°C) but a cold winter rest period is not needed. **Soil:** Standard potting mix. **Fertilization:** Feed monthly from spring through fall with half-strength fertilizer. **Propagation:** Stem cuttings may be taken from vining plants; they need warmth to root. May also be air-layered. Bushy types can be increased by treating shoots that form at the base of stems as cuttings. **Special Care:** Does best with moderate to high humidity. Mist regularly. Wash dust from foliage with damp sponge. Provide support for climbing stems; secure stems to support with twine or wire if necessary. Yellow, wilted leaves are due to overwatering. Leaves with brown edges and tips are due to low humidity. Leggy growth with small pale leaves is due to low light.

## PHLEBODIUM aureum (Rabbit's-Foot Fern, Hare's-Foot Fern, Golden Polypody, Blue Fern)

The large fronds of this durable fern are divided into spreading strap-shaped leaflets. Fronds are normally bright green, but the blue fern (top), 'Mandaianum,' offers handsome blue-green foliage. The leaves of 'Mayi' are ruffled along the edges. Also named *Polypodium aureum*, this fern's hairy creeping rhizome inspired the name rabbit's-foot fern, and the golden spore cases on the undersides of the fronds inspired the name golden polypody.

**Light:** Curtain-filtered east or west exposure, or a north window. **Water:** Keep soil moist. **Temperature:** Room temperatures; minimum of 60°F (16°C) in winter. **Soil:** Half potting soil and half peat. **Fertilization:** Feed monthly from spring through fall. **Propagation:** Divide rhizomes in spring and pin to soil surface to root. **Special Care:** Does not need high humidity.

## PHOENIX (Date Palm)

Date palms have single or multiple trunks roughened by the stubs of old leaf bases and have fine-textured foliage. Several species are grown as houseplants. *P. dactylifera*, the palm that produces edible dates, has stiff upright leaves. *P. canariensis* (middle) remains fairly compact and produces a stout trunk. The most popular one for indoors is *P. roebelenii*, the miniature date palm, since its foliage arches gracefully and the plant is slow-growing.

**Light:** Bright indirect light; some direct sun in winter. **Water:** Keep soil moist. **Temperature:** Normal room temperatures. **Soil:** Standard potting mix with dried manure added. **Fertilization:** Feed monthly in spring and summer. **Propagation:** Sow seeds or divide multiple-trunked plants. **Special Care:** Tolerates being pot-bound.

## PHYLLITIS scolopendrium (Hart's-Tongue Fern)

This unusual fern grows long strap-shaped leathery leaves from a central crown. Several varieties with wavy-edged or crinkled foliage are popular houseplants and are more commonly grown than the plain species. 'Undulata' (bottom) is admired for its wavy leaves. 'Cristata' grows less tall than the typical two feet and has ruffled leaf edges.

**Light:** A north window or interior light. **Water:** Keep soil moist. **Temperature:** Cool room temperatures, down to 50°F (10°C) at night in winter. **Soil:** Standard potting mix. **Fertilization:** Feed once in spring and once in summer with fish emulsion. **Propagation:** Divide plants in spring. **Special Care:** Needs high humidity; grow on a pebble tray or mist daily.

94

**PILEA** (Aluminum Plant, Panamiga)

These small foliage plants with their metallic colorations add spark to a collection of green plants. The aluminum plant (top), *P. cadierei*, has pointed oval leaves with bright silver markings. Its variety 'Minima' is a dwarf and grows only six inches tall. *P. involucrata*, the panamiga, has unusual leaves that are tinged dark bronze when young and are puckered and quilted into a regular pattern of tiny bumps.

**Light:** Bright indirect light. **Water:** Keep soil moist. **Temperature:** Warm room temperatures. **Soil:** Standard potting mix with extra peat. **Fertilization:** Feed once a month from spring through fall. **Propagation:** Take cuttings. **Special Care:** Pinch to promote attractive shape. Plants may lose lower leaves and look spindly as they mature; renew from cuttings.

**PIPER** (Pepper, Betel)

*P. nigrum* (middle) is the tropical vine that produces peppercorns which are ground into pepper. The leaves of its close relative, *P. betle*, are used in an Indian food called paan. Both vines make attractive houseplants with leathery, heart-shaped leaves. The pepper plant is reluctant to bloom indoors, but if it does, the flowers will be followed by green berries that change into black peppercorns.

**Light:** Bright indirect light or a north window. **Water:** Keep soil moist. **Temperature:** Warm room temperatures. **Soil:** Standard potting mix. **Fertilization:** Feed every two weeks from spring through fall. **Propagation:** Take stem cuttings and supply warmth. **Special Care:** Provide support for climbing stems. Needs moderate humidity.

**PISONIA brunoniana** (Map Plant)

This tall bushy plant is often mistaken for a variety of fig since the foliage is similar in appearance. The green-leaved form is rarely seen and the variegated variety (bottom) with long pale green leaves and broad creamy-white margins is more popular. Unlike most figs, the map plant needs moderate to high humidity or the foliage will wither.

**Light:** The variegated form needs very bright light from a curtain-filtered southern, eastern or western exposure. **Water:** Keep soil moist. **Temperature:** Warm room temperatures. **Soil:** Standard potting mix. **Fertilization:** Feed monthly from spring through fall. **Propagation:** Take stem cuttings and provide bottom heat. **Special Care:** Needs high humidity; grow small plants on a pebble tray, large plants in a humidified room. Does not rest in winter.

### PITTOSPORUM tobira (Japanese Pittosporum)

This pretty plant makes a durable indoor shrub especially suited for rooms that are cold or drafty in winter. The blunt-ended leaves are arranged in whorls at the ends of the branches and sweetly scented flowers that resemble orange blossoms appear in spring. The variegated form, offering gray-green foliage with creamy-white borders, is quite striking and equally hardy.

**Light:** Direct sun from a southern, eastern, or western exposure. **Water:** Keep soil moist. **Temperature:** Cool room temperatures, down to 40° to 50°F (4° to 10°C) at night in winter. **Soil:** Standard potting mix. **Fertilization:** Feed monthly from spring through fall. **Propagation:** Take cuttings in late summer, or air-layer. **Special Care:** Does best with moderate to high humidity.

### PLATYCERIUM (Staghorn Fern)

The fertile fronds of these bizarre-looking epiphytes are shaped like antlers and are even covered with soft white fuzz. Depending upon the species, the leaves can grow from three to ten feet long. At their bases grow round, infertile leaves which anchor the plant to its treetop location.

**Light:** Bright indirect light or a curtain-filtered eastern or western exposure. **Water:** Allow soil to almost dry between thorough waterings. **Temperature:** Warm room temperatures, down to 60°F (16°C) at night in winter; tolerates 50°F (10°C). **Soil:** Grow in a pot of pure peat moss or sphagnum, or anchor to a wad of sphagnum secured to a board or bark slab. **Fertilization:** Feed once in spring and once in summer with fish emulsion. **Propagation:** Separate pups. **Special Care:** Needs moderate humidity. Best displayed as a hanging plant.

### PLECTRANTHUS (Swedish Ivy, Candle Plant)

These are very rewarding plants to grow since they are rapid growers and in no time at all produce long trailing stems covered with beautiful glossy leaves. The candle plant (bottom), *P. oertendahlii*, features leaves decorated with silvery veins and long spikes of tiny lavender flowers. *P. australis*, Swedish ivy, is well known for its ease of culture and bright green scalloped-edged leaves.

**Light:** Bright indirect light, curtain-filtered sun, or an eastern exposure. **Water:** Keep soil moist. **Temperature:** Normal room temperatures; tolerates 55°F (13°C) at night in winter. **Soil:** Standard potting mix. **Fertilization:** Feed monthly with quarter-strength fertilizer. **Propagation:** Take stem cuttings. **Special Care:** Old plants may become ungainly; renew from cuttings or severely cut back long branches.

## PLUMBAGO auriculata (Cape Leadwort)

Throughout summer and fall, the cape leadwort is covered with clusters of white or sky-blue flowers that resemble garden phlox. The plant forms long arching stems that look best when secured to a trellis or a wire support. Cape leadwort needs lots of sun and may be grown outdoors during summer.

**Light:** Full sun from a southern exposure. **Water:** Keep soil moist. **Temperature:** Normal room temperatures during growth; during winter rest period, keep at about 50°F (10°C). **Soil:** Standard potting mix. **Fertilization:** Feed monthly from spring through fall. **Propagation:** Take cuttings in fall and provide bottom heat. **Special Care:** Cut back stems severely after flowering ceases in fall. Leaves may drop during winter if temperature is very low, but they should regrow in spring.

## PODOCARPUS macrophyllus (Buddhist Pine, Southern Yew)

Arranged in spirals around the stems, the soft, wide needles of the Buddhist pine emerge yellow-green before maturing to deep green. Branches grow upright at first and tend to bend downwards as they grow. This is an excellent indoor tree for cold, drafty spots, but it will languish if kept too warm in winter.

**Light:** Curtain-filtered eastern or western exposure. **Water:** Keep soil moist during growing season; let dry slightly in winter. **Temperature:** Cool room temperatures; needs 45° to 50°F (7° to 10°C) in winter. **Soil:** Standard potting mix. **Fertilization:** Feed monthly from spring through summer. **Propagation:** Take cuttings in fall. **Special Care:** Pinch and prune regularly to maintain compact size; prune severely in spring. Does best in a small pot.

## POLYSCIAS (Balfour Aralia, Ming Aralia)

Balfour aralia (bottom), *P. balfouriana*, and ming aralia, *P. fruticosa*, make attractive small indoor trees, but are rather difficult to grow. The balfour aralia has rounded leaflets borne in groups of three. The green-leaved form is rarely seen, the variegated ones being most popular. 'Marginata' has white-edged leaves and 'Pennockii' has gray-green foliage with dark green borders. The ming aralia has dainty fernlike foliage and comes in a dwarf form.

**Light:** Curtain-filtered east or west exposure. **Water:** Keep soil moist. **Temperature:** Warm room temperatures not below 65°F (18°C) in winter. **Soil:** Standard potting mix. **Fertilization:** Feed every three months. **Propagation:** Take stem cuttings; use rooting hormone. **Special Care:** Needs high humidity. Keep out of cold drafts.

## PRIMULA (Primrose)

In winter and spring, florists sell pots of eye-catching primroses. The plants will continue to bloom as houseplants for many months and provide welcome splashes of color only if they are kept cool, moist and out of direct sun. After flowering is finished, most primroses are best discarded, because they are difficult to grow and rebloom as houseplants.

Primroses fall into two broad groups. They may either grow as rosettes of coarse leaves hugging the soil and produce large flowers on short stalks, or they may have leafy stems topped by dense or airy clusters of blossoms. *P. polyanthus* is the most commonly grown stemless kind. Large yellow, white, blue, or purple flowers peek above the foliage. Many beautiful and brilliantly colored varieties are available. Leaves are long, coarse and spoon-shaped.

The fairy primrose (top), *P. malacoides*, is a lovely stemmed-primrose. Its airy clusters of rose, lavender-pink, or white blossoms bloom for long periods of time on elongating stalks. As long as it is kept cool, a fairy primrose will send up new flowering stalks for three or four months. The Chinese primrose (bottom), *P. sinensis*, has large yellow-eyed flowers that come in a variety of colors, and has softly hairy leaves.

Another primrose for growing indoors is *P. obconica* (middle). It is sometimes called the poison primrose because its rough leaves can cause rashes on some people who handle them. The large blossoms come in white, pink, mauve, or blue and have a greenish eye in their centers. The blooms first appear close to the foliage but as the blooming period progresses, the flowering stalk elongates and holds the flowers high. **Light:** Does best in a north window, but bright indirect light is also good. Keep out of direct sun. **Water:** Keep soil moist but not soggy. **Temperature:** Primroses must be kept very cool to prolong flowering. Temperatures of 55° to 60°F (13° to 16°C) during the day are necessary; may be kept colder during the night or during the day. **Soil:** Standard potting mix. **Fertilization:** Feed every two weeks with half-strength fertilizer. **Propagation:** Nurserymen propagate primroses by seed. For winter-blooming plants, sow seed the previous spring and keep seedlings and plants in a very cool but bright spot. **Special Care:** Moderate humidity is needed; grow plants on a pebble tray. If temperatures are higher than desirable, mist plants frequently. Yellow foliage is due to hot, dry air. A short flowering period is also due to too much heat. Removing faded flowers will help prolong blooming. *P. vulgaris* may be transplanted to the garden; others are best discarded after flowering.

98

**PSEUDERANTHEMUM** (False Eranthemum, Chocolate Plant)

These decorative tropical species are difficult to grow as houseplants because they need warmth and high humidity. Try them in a terrarium or a greenhouse. *P. sinuatum* (top) has long leaves with jagged teeth. *P. atropurpureum* offers wine-red foliage spotted with olive green, or a green-leaved form with gold veins. *P. alatum*, chocolate plant, has coppery-brown foliage. **Light:** Bright indirect light or interior light. **Water:** Keep soil moist during the growing season; allow to dry slightly in winter. **Temperature:** Warm room temperatures, not below 60°F (16°C) in winter. **Soil:** Standard potting mix. **Fertilization:** Feed monthly from spring through fall. **Propagation:** Take cuttings. **Special Care:** Must have high humidity. Renew leggy plants from cuttings.

**PTERIS** (Table Fern, Brake Fern)

Many species of this large genus of tropical and subtropical ferns make excellent, easy-to-grow houseplants. These ferns are so popular that many interesting and beautiful varieties have been bred, offering a wide selection of decorator-quality plants for fern-lovers.

Perhaps the most well-known fern of this genus is the Victoria table fern (middle), *P. ensiformis*. Its airy fronds are heavily marked with silver, leaving only a small bordering edge of blue-green. *P. quadriaurita* 'Argyraea' (bottom) has similarly marked foliage, but the leaflets are broader and more bold in texture. *P. cretica* 'Albo-Lineata' has creamy stripes running down the middle of its straight-edged leaflets. The varieties 'Distinction' and 'Wilsonii' are novelty plants with oddly shaped foliage.

Though they aren't difficult ferns to grow, table ferns and brake ferns need moderately high humidity and very bright light to do well indoors. Direct sun or low humidity will quickly be the end of these elegant ferns.

**Light:** Bright indirect light or curtain-filtered eastern exposure; keep out of direct sun. **Water:** Keep soil moist. **Temperature:** Normal room temperatures, with nights in winter about 55°F (13°C). **Soil:** Standard potting mix with extra peat. **Propagation:** Divide plants in spring. **Special Care:** Needs high humidity. Mist several times daily and grow on a pebble tray, or grow in a humidified room. Brown leaf tips and edges are due to low humidity.

### REBUTIA (Crown Cactus)

The smallest plants in the cactus family, crown cacti form globes only a few inches across, though individual plants may grow as clusters of several small spiny balls. The blossoms emerge from the bases of the stems and tower above the plant. Blossoms are usually red and appear from spring through summer.

**Light:** Four hours of direct sun a day, but shade from intense noon sun in summer. **Water:** Allow soil to dry somewhat between waterings from spring through fall. Let dry thoroughly in winter. **Temperature:** Keep at 40° to 45°F (4° to 7°C) at night in winter; normal room temperatures the rest of the year. **Soil:** Cactus/succulent mix. **Fertilization:** Feed once in spring with low-nitrogen fertilizer. **Propagation:** Separate offsets. **Special Care:** Keep cool until flower buds are visible.

### RECHSTEINERIA (Brazilian Edelweiss, Cardinal Flower)

These gesneriads feature large hairy leaves on stems about a foot tall or in rosettes, and clusters of tubular flowers. *R. leucotricha*, Brazilian edelweiss, has leaves covered with dense white hairs and salmon-red flowers. Cardinal flower (middle), *R. cardinalis*, often blooms in midwinter, showing off red, fuzzy flowers against velvety green foliage. The many species of *Rechsteineria* may be listed as *Sinningia*.

**Light:** Bright indirect light or a north window. **Water:** Allow soil to dry slightly between waterings. **Temperature:** Warm room temperatures. **Soil:** Standard potting mix with extra peat. **Fertilization:** Feed every two weeks with high-phosphorus fertilizer. **Propagation:** Take stem or leaf cuttings, or divide tuber. **Special Care:** Needs high humidity; grow on a pebble tray.

### RHAPHIDOPHORA aurea (Pothos, Devil's Ivy)

Pothos can be grown in a hanging container, trained to grow up a moss-covered support, or allowed to trail across a mantlepiece or tabletop. The stems often reach three feet long and the leathery pointed leaves come in several beautifully variegated forms. 'Marble Queen' (bottom) has irregular creamy-white markings. 'Tricolor' is marked with deep yellow, cream and pale green. Pothos may be listed in the genera *Scindapsus* and *Epipremnum*.

**Light:** Variegations are best in curtain-filtered or bright indirect light; also grows in interior light. **Water:** Allow soil to dry somewhat during growth; let dry more in winter. **Temperature:** Warm room temperatures. **Soil:** Standard potting mix. **Fertilization:** Feed monthly during growth. **Propagation:** Stem cuttings. **Special Care:** Wash foliage occasionally.

## RHIPSALIDOPSIS gaertneri (Easter Cactus)

This freely blooming cactus puts on its show each spring, which accounts for the name Easter cactus. Beautiful bright red or pink flowers are borne at the ends of the branches on plants that receive light only during the daylight hours. These jungle cacti have no thorns and need much more moisture than other cacti. 'Crimson Grant' blooms in spring and again in fall.

**Light:** Bright indirect light. **Water:** Allow soil to dry slightly between waterings during growth; let dry more during winter. **Temperature:** Needs night temperatures below 65°F (18°C) to encourage flower formation. **Soil:** Standard potting mix. **Fertilization:** Feed every two weeks from spring through summer with half-strength fertilizer. **Propagation:** Stem cuttings. **Special Care:** Plants need to have light and dark according to the natural day length to flower.

## RHODODENDRON (Azalea)

Though they naturally flower in the spring, azaleas are offered for sale in full bloom by florists from Thanksgiving to Easter. Such florist azaleas are forced into bloom in a greenhouse, but this doesn't seem to affect the plants' vigor. With proper care you can keep an azalea and bring it into flower again year after year, though without special treatment it will flower only in spring.

Florist azaleas are usually hybrids of the frost-tender *R. indicum* (once classified in the genus *Azalea*). Their flaring funnel-shaped flowers come in shades of pink, violet, magenta and white, and bicolored ones are available too. It's best to purchase a plant with tight flower buds—that way you'll be sure to get a long blooming period. After flowers fade, azaleas make attractive fine-textured foliage plants.

**Light:** An eastern exposure is best. **Water:** Keep soil moist; do not let dry out. **Temperature:** Needs temperatures of 45° to 55°F (7° to 13°C) during the night in fall and winter; normal room temperatures, though coolness is preferred, the rest of the time. **Soil:** Standard potting mix with extra peat. **Fertilization:** Feed in spring after flowers drop, again a month later, and once more in midsummer with fertilizer designed for acid-loving plants. **Propagation:** Take cuttings from new growth in spring. **Special Care:** Remove faded flowers. Mist foliage occasionally. Grows best if plant is placed in a shady spot in the garden with the pot sunk in the ground from late spring until frost threatens in fall.

## RHOEO spathacea (Moses-In-A-Boat, Purple-Leaved Spiderwort)

The flowers of this colorful foliage plant are the inspiration for the common name Moses-in-a-boat—the tiny white flowers barely peek from inside two shell-shaped bracts. Though the blossoms are a curiosity, the plant is grown primarily for its foliage. The long fleshy leaves are metallic olive-green on top and glossy purple beneath. The variety 'Vittata' (top) is striped with pale yellow on top.

**Light:** Bright indirect light. **Water:** Keep soil moist during growth; allow to dry somewhat in winter. **Temperature:** Normal room temperatures. **Soil:** Standard potting mix with extra peat. **Fertilization:** Feed monthly from spring through fall. **Propagation:** Use side shoots as cuttings. **Special Care:** Needs high humidity; mist frequently.

## RHOICISSUS capensis (Cape Grape, Evergreen Grape)

The cape grape resembles a grapevine even more than its close relative the grape ivy. The round leaves are lobed and coarsely toothed, closely resembling actual grape leaves. Rusty hairs coat the leaf undersides and the stems. Cape grape is a robust plant suited for a hanging container, or for training onto a trellis or other support. The small purplish-red berries are edible.

**Light:** Bright indirect light or morning sun. **Water:** Allow soil to dry somewhat between waterings. **Temperature:** Normal room temperatures; 45° to 50°F (7° to 10°C) in winter. **Soil:** Standard potting soil. **Fertilization:** Feed monthly during growing season. **Propagation:** Take stem cuttings in spring or summer. **Special Care:** Cut back leggy plants in spring. Provide support for tendril-bearing stems if desired.

## SAINTPAULIA ionantha (African Violet)

When grown correctly, African violets bloom year-round, producing bouquets of white, blue, purple, pink, lavender, magenta, or bicolored blooms in a mound above a symmetrical rosette of velvety leaves. Leaves of some varieties have deep purple undersides and others are variegated with creamy-white. Providing the proper levels of moisture and light is the key to growing these plants successfully.

**Light:** Curtain-filtered east or west exposure, or a north window. **Water:** Allow soil to dry somewhat between waterings. **Temperature:** Warm room temperatures. **Soil:** Standard potting soil with extra peat. **Fertilization:** Feed every two weeks with high-phosphorus fertilizer. **Propagation:** Take leaf cuttings. **Special Care:** Pinch off any side shoots. Outer leaves droop and wilt if fertilizer salts build up on side of pot.

**SANSEVIERIA trifasciata** (Snake Plant, Mother-In-Law's Tongue, Sansevieria, Bird's-Nest Sansevieria)

Perhaps the easiest and most widely grown houseplants of all, snake plants withstand all kinds of ill-treatment and neglect. The stiff leathery leaves are semi-succulent so they are quite durable under low humidity and drought conditions. The plants even withstand cold drafts and dim light. Just about the only thing that bothers a snake plant is too much water—soggy soil rots the roots in no time at all.

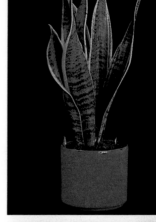

The most popular snake plant is 'Laurentii' (top), which has sword-shaped green leaves banded with gray-green and edged with a distinct yellow border. 'Bantels Sensation' has golden bands and white stripes, but individual leaves of the same plant may have different markings.

The bird's-nest sansevieria (middle), 'Hahnii,' has very short leaves forming a deep vase with flared sides. 'Golden Hahnii' has leaves variegated like those of 'Laurentii.' 'Silver Hahnii Marginata' offers silvery-green-hued foliage with dark green bands and creamy yellow margins.

**Light:** Does best in bright indirect light, but thrives even in dim interior light. **Water:** Allow soil to dry between waterings. **Temperature:** Normal room temperatures are best, but tolerates 55°F (13°C) in winter. **Soil:** Standard potting mix or cactus/succulent mix. **Fertilization:** Feed monthly with half-strength fertilizer from spring through fall. **Propagation:** Divide plants in spring or make leaf segment cuttings. Variegated plants may loose markings if propagated by cuttings. **Special Care:** Wash leaves periodically.

**SAUROMATUM guttatum** (Voodoo Lily)

This weird plant is grown purely as a curiosity—it can hardly be thought attractive-looking and it gives off a horrible smell! Simply sit the fat tuber on a windowsill without any soil at all, and a tall spike that unfolds into a blossom—a two-and-a-half-foot-tall purple-spotted petallike bract curling around a column studded with tiny white flowers—will emerge. After the flower withers, plant the tuber in soil and a single long-stalked divided leaf appears.

**Light:** Full sun while in growth. **Water:** After tuber is planted, allow soil to dry somewhat between waterings. **Temperature:** Warm room temperatures during growth. **Soil:** Standard potting mix. **Fertilization:** Feed monthly with quarter-strength fertilizer. **Propagation:** Divide offsets. **Special Care:** Withhold water in fall until leaf dies. Place tuber in cool, dark spot until winter.

103

**SAXIFRAGA stolonifera** (Strawberry Begonia, Strawberry Geranium)

These charming hanging plants grow as mounds of soil-hugging round leaves that send out long fragile runners from which dangle tiny new plants. A well-grown plant will have numerous runners and baby plants. Foliage is dark green with white veins and red undersides. The variety 'Tricolor' has green-and-white-variegated leaves with pink edges and rose undersides. In midsummer, tall stalks of airy white flowers grow from the main plant.

**Light:** A north window or bright indirect light. **Water:** Allow soil to dry slightly between waterings. **Temperature:** Cool room temperatures are best. **Soil:** Standard potting mix. **Fertilization:** Feed once in spring and once in summer. **Propagation:** Root dangling plants. **Special Care:** Mist occasionally.

**SCHEFFLERA** (Umbrella Tree)

The umbrella tree is a good choice where a large tropical floor plant is needed. The long-stalked leaves are divided into seven or more segments and arranged like fingers on a hand. *S. actinophylla*, frequently named *Brassaia actinophylla*, is the most popular species. It usually forms a single trunk and can grow quite tall, but can be kept bushier if the stem tips are pruned. *S. digitata* is similar, but has toothed leaves.

**Light:** Does best with full sun but tolerates low interior light. **Water:** Allow soil to dry somewhat between waterings. **Temperature:** Warm room temperatures. **Soil:** Standard potting mix. **Fertilization:** Feed monthly from spring through fall if grown in full sun; less often in low light. **Propagation:** Air-layer tall plants. **Special Care:** Foliage will droop if plant is kept cold and wet.

**SCINDAPSUS pictus** (Satin Pothos)

This pretty plant is a tropical climber related to devil's ivy or pothos, and indeed they are both often classified in the same genus. The dark green foliage is splotched with gray-green on top, and colored very pale green on the undersides. 'Argyraeus' (bottom) has silver spots and is more commonly grown than the species. Satin pothos makes a handsome plant when allowed to trail along a surface or cascade from a hanging basket. It can also be trained to a support.

**Light:** Bright indirect light. **Water:** Allow soil to dry somewhat between waterings. **Temperature:** Warm room temperatures; down to 65°F (18°C) at night in winter. **Soil:** Standard potting mix. **Fertilization:** Feed once a month in spring and summer. **Propagation:** Take stem cuttings anytime. **Special Care:** Provide moss-covered support for a climbing plant.

## SCIRPUS cernuus (Club Rush)

Club rush, a native of wet meadows or boggy places, makes an unusual houseplant. If kept very wet, its tufts of floppy grassy foliage will stay bright green—allow it to dry out and the plant will brown rapidly. It is so fond of water in fact that, though the procedure would kill most plants, leaving the pot standing in a saucer of water is the best way to keep a club rush happy.

**Light:** Bright indirect light or an eastern exposure. **Water:** Keep soil wet. **Temperature:** Normal room temperatures are fine. **Soil:** Standard potting mix. **Fertilization:** Feed monthly from spring through fall. **Propagation:** Divide plants by cutting through the root-ball in spring. **Special Care:** Leaves may be cut off at soil level in spring to make room for new growth. Mist frequently.

## SEDUM (Sedum, Stonecrop, Burro's-Tail, Jelly-Beans)

About twenty species of this diverse genus of succulents are grown as houseplants. They offer beautifully colored fleshy leaves, which may be cylindrical or flat, and fluffy springtime flower heads borne on tall stems. Sedums may be trailing or upright and usually have brittle stems. Leaves are easily dislodged from the stem and root readily if they fall on the soil.

*S. morganianum*, burro's-tail, is a favorite sedum. It has cylindrical blue-green leaves that end in sharp points and are arranged so tightly on the stems that they appear braided. Burro's-tail makes a stunning display when grown in a hanging container, and if it is suspended out of the way, its fragile stems can come to no harm.

*S. dendroideum* (middle) is also blue-green, but it is upright-growing. When grown in full sun, the leaves become tinged with red. *S. griseum* (bottom) has very thin pointed leaves and upright stems. A very colorful creeping plant is *S. rubrotinctum*, jelly beans. It gets its name because its red-tinged green leaves are shiny and fat, shaped just like the candy, jelly beans.

**Light:** At least four hours of direct sun a day. **Water:** Allow soil to dry somewhat between waterings during the growing season; water only enough to keep from shriveling in winter. **Temperature:** Does best with night temperatures about 60°F (16°C) during the growing season and 45°F (7°C) in winter. **Soil:** Standard cactus/succulent mix. **Fertilization:** Repot annually and give no fertilizer, or feed once in spring and once in summer with low-nitrogen fertilizer. **Propagation:** Take leaf or stem cuttings. **Special Care:** Repot burro's-tail only when absolutely necessary since it has very fragile stems.

## SENECIO (Cineraria)

When fresh and full of flowers, this florist plant (*S. hybridus*) is simply stunning. A mound of large daisy-like flowers tops the foliage and the colors are magnificent shades of clear blue, purple, lavender, red, magenta and pink. The velvety blossoms are set off by a bright white ring around their buttonlike centers. Cinerarias are annuals and will not flower again, so discard the plant after the flowers fade.

**Light:** Bright indirect light. **Water:** Keep soil moist, and water from beneath to avoid wetting the crown. **Temperature:** Keep as cool as possible to prolong the flowers; about 50°F (10°C) is ideal. **Soil:** No need to repot. **Fertilization:** Feeding is not necessary. **Propagation:** Nurserymen sow seeds in late summer and grow the seedlings in a cool greenhouse. **Special Care:** Aphids may be a problem.

## SENECIO (String-of-Beads, Gooseberry Kleinia)

Several succulent species of *Senecio* are charming plants for hanging containers. Their thin trailing stems are studded with globular green leaves. Gooseberry kleinia (middle), *S. herreianus*, has pointed leaves with translucent bands, giving it a resemblance to gooseberries. *S. rowleyanus* has leaves as round as peas and with a single translucent band.

**Light:** At least four hours of direct sun a day. **Water:** Allow soil to dry somewhat between waterings. **Temperature:** Normal room temperatures, with winter nights 50° to 55°F (10° to 13°C). **Soil:** Standard cactus/succulent mix. **Fertilization:** Feed once in spring and once in summer with low-nitrogen fertilizer. **Propagation:** Cut off several inches of stem and lay on soil surface. **Special Care:** Cut back long stems.

## SENECIO (Parlor Ivy, German Ivy, Natal Ivy)

Two semi-succulent species of *Senecio* bear a remarkable resemblance to English ivy. *S. macroglossus*, natal ivy, has fleshy leaves and trailing stems and, in a most un-ivylike fashion, produces large showy yellow flowers in summer. Its variety 'Variegata' (bottom) has green-and-white variegated leaves. *S. mikanioides*, called parlor ivy or German ivy, is similar in appearance but does not produce showy flowers.

**Light:** Bright indirect light or some morning sun. **Water:** Allow soil to dry somewhat between waterings. **Temperature:** Cool room temperatures, down to 40° to 50°F (4° to 10°C) at night. **Soil:** Standard potting mix. **Fertilization:** Feed every two weeks with half-strength fertilizer during growth. **Propagation:** Take stem cuttings. **Special Care:** Best displayed in a hanging basket.

### SETCREASEA purpurea (Purple Heart)

When grown in good light, this foliage plant is a deep purple all over! Slightly fuzzy and closely clasping the pliant stems, the leaves are strap-shaped and end in points. Tiny pink flowers, each lasting only one day, appear at the stem tips throughout the summer. Stems grow upright at first and then bend gracefully downwards, making the plant especially appealing in a hanging basket.

**Light:** Several hours of full sun for best foliage color; leaves will be greenish in bright indirect light. **Water:** Allow soil to dry somewhat between waterings. **Temperature:** Normal room temperatures. **Soil:** Standard potting mix. **Fertilization:** Feed monthly with half-strength fertilizer. **Propagation:** Take stem cuttings. **Special Care:** Does best with moderate humidity.

### SIDERASIS fuscata (Brown Spiderwort)

The brown spiderwort is not one for amateurs. It needs warmth and high humidity, and it is finicky about its watering. If you can keep it happy, brown spiderwort will reward you with a spreading rosette of olive-green leaves that are covered with shiny brown hairs, marked with a silver stripe down their centers, and colored purple on their undersides. Well-grown plants produce small lavender-blue flowers.

**Light:** Bright indirect light. **Water:** Allow soil to dry somewhat between waterings. **Temperature:** Warm room temperatures above 60°F (16°C) in winter. **Soil:** Standard potting mix. **Fertilization:** Feed once a month with quarter-strength fertilizer. **Propagation:** Divide plants in spring or summer. **Special Care:** Needs high humidity; do not mist, but grow on a pebble tray.

### SINNINGIA speciosa (Gloxinia)

The huge bell-shaped flowers of a gloxinia are the texture of velvet and are borne from the center of a compact cluster of soft hairy leaves. Most gloxinias grown today are hybrids and come in an array of beautiful colors and are often speckled or rimmed with contrasting colors. Gloxinias grow from tubers and go through a yearly cycle of growth and dormancy. They can be made to bloom at almost any time of the year.

**Light:** Curtain-filtered eastern exposure. **Water:** Keep soil moist. **Temperature:** Warm room temperatures. **Soil:** Standard potting mix. **Fertilization:** Feed once a week with quarter-strength fertilizer. **Propagation:** Leaf cuttings. **Special Care:** After flowering stops, withhold water until foliage dies, then store in dark, warm spot for two to four months, or until new shoots appear. Then move into good light and resume care.

### SKIMMIA japonica (Japanese Skimmia)

This garden shrub is often sold as a houseplant by florists because it has such attractive red berries. The berries will last for months and are preceded by fluffy clusters of white flowers in spring. Only female plants have berries, and the flowers must be pollinated by a male plant if the berries are to form at all. The variety 'Nana,' a compact, slow-growing plant, is usually the one sold as a houseplant.

**Light:** An eastern exposure. **Water:** Keep soil moist. **Temperature:** Normal room temperatures; about 45°F (7°C) in fall and winter. **Soil:** Standard potting mix. **Fertilization:** Feed once in spring and once in summer. **Propagation:** Take cuttings in spring from new growth; use rooting hormone. **Special Care:** If leaves yellow, feed with fertilizer made for acid-loving plants.

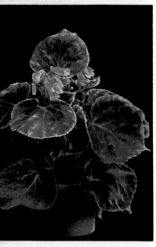

### SMITHIANTHA (Temple-Bells)

Like many gesneriads, temple-bells grows from a scaly rhizome and has a yearly cycle of growth and dormancy. The velvety leaves begin growing in spring and stalks of bell-shaped flowers appear from late summer until winter. Many beautiful hybrids offering speckled flowers in white and all shades of pink, red, orange, or yellow, and offering foliage marbled with red or purple are available.

**Light:** Curtain-filtered eastern exposure. **Water:** Keep soil moist during growth; water slightly during dormancy. **Temperature:** Warm room temperatures not below 65°F (18°C) in winter. **Soil:** Standard potting mix with extra peat. **Fertilization:** Feed monthly during growth. **Propagation:** Take stemless leaf cuttings or divide rhizomes. **Special Care:** Needs high humidity; grow on pebble tray.

### SOLANUM pseudocapsicum (Jerusalem Cherry)

Admired for its gleaming orange-red berries that resemble cherries, the Jerusalem cherry is actually a relative of the tomato, though its fruit is poisonous. It makes a festive houseplant in winter when the berries are ripe. White flowers appear throughout the summer, turning into green berries that ripen to red or yellow in fall.

**Light:** An eastern exposure. **Water:** Keep soil moist. **Temperature:** For longest lasting fruit, keep at about 60°F (16°C) or cooler. **Soil:** Standard potting mix. **Fertilization:** Feed monthly. **Propagation:** Take stem cuttings in spring or sow seed. **Special Care:** Plants usually live for only one or two seasons. Cut back severely in spring. Leaves may drop from overwatering. Berries drop if light is too low.

**SOLEIROLIA soleirolii** (Baby's-Tears, Irish Moss)
This dainty creeping plant is an ideal plant to use in a miniature landscape, as a groundcover in the pot of a large plant, or as an adorable miniature. Its threadlike stems are covered with mats of tiny heart-shaped leaves and greenish flowers, and grow so prolifically that they spill over the edge of the pot in no time.
**Light:** Bright indirect light or north light. **Water:** Keep soil moist. **Temperature:** Cool room temperatures. **Soil:** Standard potting mix with extra peat. **Fertilization:** Feed monthly with half-strength fertilizer. **Propagation:** Divide plants when centers become bare. **Special Care:** Does best with high humidity; mist leaves several times daily, or grow in a terrarium.

**SONERILA margaritacea** (Pearly Sonerila, Frosted Sonerila)
Unfortunately for the plant-lover, this dazzling tropical foliage plant is exceedingly difficult to grow outside of a greenhouse. Warmth and high humidity are musts, so the winter months are usually its doom. You can try showing off the silver-coated, coppery-green leaves in a bottle garden or a terrarium, where the humidity should be sufficient. If the plant thrives, it will produce small rose flowers.
**Light:** Bright indirect light. **Water:** Keep soil moist. **Temperature:** Warm room temperatures above 60°F (16°C). **Soil:** Standard potting mix with extra peat. **Fertilization:** Feed monthly from spring through fall with half-strength fertilizer. **Propagation:** Take stem cuttings. **Special Care:** Brown leaf tips are due to low humidity. Leaf drop is due to cold temperatures.

**SPARMANNIA africana** (African Linden)
A very popular houseplant in Europe, African linden isn't well-known in America. It grows into a three-foot-tall, bushy plant with large, bold-textured leaves. The heart-shaped foliage feels like felt because downy hairs cover the upper and lower surfaces of the leaves. Clusters of small white flowers with yellow centers appear in spring. 'Flore Pleno' is a double-flowered variety.
**Light:** Full sun in winter; bright indirect light the rest of the year. **Water:** Keep soil moist. Needs large quantities of water in summer. **Temperature:** Normal room temperatures. **Soil:** Standard potting mix. **Fertilization:** Feed monthly. **Propagation:** Take cuttings from the flowering stems in spring. **Special Care:** Pinch and prune regularly to maintain attractive shape. Prune severely after flowering.

## SPATHIPHYLLUM (Peace Lily)

Though it looks exotic and hard to grow, the peace lily readily blooms indoors as long as you can keep it warm enough in winter. The glossy oblong leaves are dark green and grow directly from the soil, forming thick clumps of foliage. For months in spring, and often again in fall, stalks bearing large, white waxy bracts and spires of tiny flowers appear.

**Light:** Bright indirect to low light. No direct sun. **Water:** Keep soil moist. **Temperature:** Warm room temperatures above 60°F (16°C). **Soil:** One-part standard potting mix combined with one-part fir bark. **Fertilization:** Feed every two weeks with half-strength fertilizer. **Propagation:** Divide plants in spring. **Special Care:** Repot every two years. Keep humidity high; grow on a pebble tray and syringe leaves.

## SPREKELIA formosissima (Aztec Lily)

In May or June, sometimes even before any leaves appear, the Aztec lily produces a tall flowering stalk topped with a brilliant red, orchidlike blossom. Large bulbs may have two flowering stalks. After the flower fades, the strap-shaped leaves remain green and nourish the bulb until dormancy begins in the fall. By giving alternating periods of moisture and drought, Aztec lily can be made to bloom more than once a year.

**Light:** Four hours of direct sun. **Water:** Keep soil moist during growth, dry during dormancy. **Temperature:** Warm room temperatures. **Soil:** Standard potting mix. **Fertilization:** Feed monthly during growth. **Propagation:** Divide bulbs when repotting. **Special Care:** Repot every three or four years. Withhold water and fertilizer to make bulb go dormant.

## STAPELIA (Starfish Plant, Carrion Flower)

Don't put your nose near the bizarre-looking blossoms of the starfish plant—they have such a foul odor that they are pollinated by flies. The enormous flowers are shaped like a star and are creamy-white with purple spots. Blooming in late summer, the rest of the year this succulent is an innocuous clump of fleshy stems. Several species are grown.

**Light:** Four hours of direct sun. **Water:** Allow soil to dry somewhat between waterings from spring through fall; in winter, water only once or twice. **Temperature:** Normal room temperatures, except in winter when must have 45°F (7°C). **Soil:** Standard potting mix with dried manure added. **Fertilization:** Feed once in spring with low-nitrogen fertilizer. **Propagation:** Take stem cuttings. **Special Care:** Blossoming plants may be kept outdoors.

110

**STENANDRIUM lindenii** (Stenandrium)
Like its relative the zebra plant, stenandrium is admired for its colorful foliage and spikes of yellow flowers. The broad, oval leaves grow on spreading stems and are dark green on top and marked along the veins with bright white or yellow. The undersides of the leaves are a pretty purplish-green. Stenandrium is a difficult plant to keep because it demands warmth and high humidity.
**Light:** Bright indirect light with some direct sun in winter; no direct sun in summer. **Water:** Keep soil moist. **Temperature:** Warm room temperatures not below 60°F (16°C). **Soil:** Standard potting mix with extra peat added. **Fertilization:** Feed monthly from spring through fall. **Propagation:** Take stem cuttings in spring. **Special Care:** Grow on a pebble tray and group with other plants to keep humidity high.

**STENOCARPUS sinuatus** (Wheel-of-Fire)
The foot-long leaves of the wheel-of-fire are shaped rather like huge oak leaves. They have a leathery texture and are colored light green on top and even paler green beneath. Growing slowly into a large tree suitable for a tub on a sunporch, wheel-of-fire is a difficult plant to keep as an ordinary houseplant. It will only produce its dramatic wheels of scarlet flowers indoors where you can provide the proper conditions.
**Light:** Full sun in winter; curtain-filtered light in summer. **Water:** Keep soil moist during growth, drier in winter. **Temperature:** Needs about 40°F (4°C) in winter. **Soil:** Standard potting mix with extra loam. **Fertilization:** Feed monthly during growth. **Propagation:** Take stem cuttings in August; keep cool all winter until rooted. **Special Care:** Summer outdoors.

**STEPHANOTIS floribunda** (Stephanotis, Madagascar Jasmine)
The exquisite flowers of stephanotis are traditional blossoms for a bride's bouquet. Waxy, white and tubular, the flowers emit an intensely sweet fragrance. They appear in clusters along the vines from spring into summer if the plant is kept cool in winter. The twining vines have widely spaced pairs of waxy leaves and must be trained to a wire trellis.
**Light:** Direct sun in winter; curtain-filtered in summer. **Water:** Keep moist during growth, drier in winter. **Temperature:** Normal room temperatures during growth; must have 55°F (13°C) in winter. **Soil:** Standard potting mix with extra loam. **Fertilization:** Feed once a month from spring through fall. **Propagation:** Take cuttings in spring and keep warm. **Special Care:** Must have high humidity. Mist several times daily.

111

**STREPTOCARPUS hybridus** (Cape Primrose)
Less common than the African violet, its relative the cape primrose is easier to grow and is just as free-blooming. Clusters of trumpet-shaped blossoms appear on slender stalks from spring through fall. Colors include white, pink, violet, purple, blue, lavender and bicolors. The Wiesmoor hybrids make outstanding houseplants—compact, rugged and floriferous.
**Light:** An east exposure is ideal. **Water:** Allow soil to dry somewhat between waterings. **Temperature:** Room temperatures; 60° to 65°F (16° to 18°C) is best in winter. Colder temperatures are tolerated. **Soil:** Standard potting mix. **Fertilization:** Feed every two weeks with high-phosphorus fertilizer. **Propagation:** Divide plants in spring. Make leaf cuttings by removing leaf, slicing into the midrib and pinning to soil. **Special Care:** Grow on a pebble tray. Cut off faded flower stalks.

**STROMANTHE** (Stromanthe)
Similar in appearance to the prayer plant and the peacock plant, stromanthe is related to both and it is just as difficult to grow. The delicate-looking foliage of *S. amabilis* (middle) is bright green on top and marked with dark green feathery stripes. *S. porteana* has silvery-white stripes on top and purple undersides. The leaves of *S. sanguinea* are solid green on top and colored purple or marked with green stripes beneath.
**Light:** Bright indirect light. **Water:** Keep soil moist but do not overwater in winter. **Temperature:** Warm room temperatures not below 60°F (16°C). **Soil:** Standard potting mix with extra peat. **Fertilization:** Feed every two weeks from spring through fall. **Propagation:** Take stem cuttings. **Special Care:** Needs high humidity. Mist leaves daily and grow on a pebble tray.

**SYNGONIUM podophyllum** (Nephthytis, Arrowhead Vine)
This philodendron relative changes shape as it matures. Young plants produce arrowhead-shaped foliage and plants are full and bushy. As the plants mature, the stems begin to vine and will climb or trail to great lengths. The foliage also changes shape and becomes divided at first into three and then into five pointed lobes. Many variegated varieties are grown.
**Light:** Bright indirect light for variegated forms; green forms tolerate low interior light. **Water:** Keep soil moist. **Temperature:** Warm room temperatures above 60°F (16°C). **Soil:** Standard potting mix. **Fertilization:** Feed once a month during growth. **Propagation:** Take stem cuttings with aerial roots. **Special Care:** Needs high humidity; mist foliage. Provide moss-covered support. To keep bushy, remove vining stems.

**TETRASTIGMA voinierianum** (Chestnut Vine)
The coarse five-lobed leaves of this relative of the popular grape ivy are shaped like chestnut leaves—the reason for the common name. A rampant vine that climbs by tendrils, the chestnut vine needs a tall, wide trellis where it will grow into a living screen. The vines can be trained to cover a picture window or sliding glass doors where privacy is desired.
**Light:** Bright indirect light or a north window. **Water:** Keep soil moist from spring through fall; allow to dry somewhat in winter. **Temperature:** Cool room temperatures, down to 50°F (10°C) in winter. **Soil:** Standard potting mix. **Fertilization:** Feed monthly during growth. **Propagation:** Take cuttings from new growth. **Special Care:** Brown leaf tips are due to dry air. Spotted and curled lower leaves which drop off are due to underwatering.

**THUNBERGIA alata** (Black-Eyed Susan Vine)
In a sunny spot, this vine blooms nonstop, producing gold, orange, white, or tan blossoms set off by dark purple or black centers. The twining stems will grow to several feet long and form a thick cover on a trellis. It is also quite pretty when grown in a hanging container. Though usually treated as an annual in the garden, black-eyed Susan vine is a tender perennial and will live for several years as a houseplant.
**Light:** Four hours of direct sun a day. **Water:** Keep soil moist. **Temperature:** Normal room temperatures. **Soil:** Standard potting mix. **Fertilization:** Feed every two weeks during growth. **Propagation:** Sow seeds and keep warm. **Special Care:** To encourage blooming, remove faded flowers before seeds are set. Discard overgrown plants and start anew.

**TILLANDSIA** (Tillandsia, Spanish Moss)
The colorful paddle-shaped flowering stalk of *T. lindenii* (bottom) produces a single orchidlike flower at a time. After one fragrant flower fades, another appears, from fall through spring. *T. cyanea* has a vivid red stalk and deep violet-blue flowers. *T. usneoides*, Spanish moss, festoons tree branches in the southern United States with its weird blue-green masses of linear leaves. It makes a novelty houseplant since it needs no soil.
**Light:** Bright indirect light or curtain-filtered light. **Water:** Keep soil moist. **Temperature:** Warm room temperatures. **Soil:** Standard potting mix with extra peat. **Fertilization:** Feed once a month with quarter-strength fertilizer applied to moist soil. **Propagation:** Separate offsets. **Special Care:** Needs high humidity. Keep Spanish moss dripping wet.

113

### TOLMIEA menziesii (Piggyback Plant)

From the center of each mature leaf of a piggyback plant sprouts a tiny new plant consisting of two miniature leaves. This fascinating habit makes this foliage plant fun to grow and propagate. Its long-stemmed bright green leaves form a large attractive mound. The plant will flourish for months, but then may suddenly decline—such sudden plant death is usually due to fluoridated water.

**Light:** Bright indirect or curtain-filtered light is best, but accepts low interior light. **Water:** Keep soil moist. **Temperature:** Normal room temperatures; down to 50°F (10°C) in winter. **Soil:** Standard potting mix. **Fertilization:** Feed every two months during growth. **Propagation:** Pin leaf bearing a plantlet to soil until roots form. **Special Care:** Water with rainwater or distilled water where tap water is fluoridated.

### TORENIA fournieri (Wishbone Flower)

A favorite garden annual for cool, shady spots, wishbone flower makes a tidy winter-blooming plant for a windowsill. The tubular flowers have two lips and are pale violet tipped with dark purple, and have yellow spots in their throats. A white-flowered variety is also available. Since wishbone flower is an annual, it will put on a lavish show of blossoms for several months, but then the plant will die.

**Light:** Curtain-filtered sun. **Water:** Keep soil moist. **Temperature:** Normal room temperatures above 60°F (16°C) for best blooming. **Soil:** Standard potting mix. **Fertilization:** Feed every two weeks. **Propagation:** Sow seeds in late summer for winter bloom. **Special Care:** Remove faded flowers before they set seed.

### TRADESCANTIA (Wandering Jew, Inch Plant)

These popular trailing plants are so easy to propagate that most people acquire them as cuttings from a friend. *P. albiflora* has dark shiny green leaves, but several variegated varieties are grown: 'Albovittata' (bottom) has white-striped leaves and 'Laekenensis' is striped with white and purple. *T. blossfeldiana* has leaves that are green on top and purple underneath. Its variety 'Variegata' produces solid green, white and purple foliage on the same plant. *T. sillamontana* has fuzzy gray-green leaves.

**Light:** Bright indirect or curtain-filtered light. **Water:** Keep moist during growth; allow to dry somewhat in winter. **Temperature:** Normal room temperatures. **Soil:** Standard potting mix. **Fertilization:** Feed every two months during growth. **Propagation:** Take stem cuttings. **Special Care:** Cut back leggy growth.

114

## TULIPA hybrida (Tulip)

Blooming indoors on a windowsill on a cold, snowy winter day, these stately spring-flowering bulbs are a welcome sight. Plant the bulbs in fall and give them several months of cold to induce flowering. Hybrid tulips come in an array of colors. For best results select those recommended for forcing.

**Light:** Keep dormant bulbs dark; when in growth, keep in curtain-filtered southern exposure. **Water:** Keep soil moist but not soggy. **Temperature:** When in growth and flower, keep at cool room temperatures. **Soil:** Standard potting mix. **Fertilization:** Not necessary. **Propagation:** Do not increase bulbs. **Special Care:** Plant bulbs in a shallow pot in fall and keep dark at about 45°F (7°C)—or in the refrigerator—for 13 weeks, then move to room temperatures in a sunny spot. Plant bulbs in garden after foliage fades.

## VALLOTA speciosa (Scarborough Lily)

The scarborough lily is an elegant bulbous plant related to the amaryllis. Its clusters of scarlet flowers appear in late summer or early fall and last for weeks if kept cool. White- and salmon-flowered varieties are available but are harder to find. The strap-shaped foliage is evergreen, unlike the amaryllis's, though the bulb rests in winter.

**Light:** Four hours of direct sun a day. **Water:** Keep soil moist during growth; allow to dry somewhat between waterings in winter. **Temperature:** Cool room temperatures down to 50°F (10°C) in winter. **Soil:** Standard potting mix with extra loam. **Fertilization:** Feed monthly from spring until flowers fade in fall. **Propagation:** Divide bulbs every three years. **Special Care:** Cut off dead flowering stalk.

## VANDA (Vanda, Blue Orchid)

These exquisite orchids are very difficult to grow as houseplants since they need much higher humidity than people find comfortable. Grow them in a warm or temperate greenhouse. Many hybrids and species are cultivated, but only a few are suitable for amateurs. The blue orchid (bottom), *V. coerulea*, produces beautiful pale or dark blue flowers in late summer or fall. *V. tricolor* has brown-spotted yellow flowers, and its variety 'Suavis' has white blooms with purple stripes.

**Light:** Southern exposure; shade from noon sun. **Water:** Keep soil moist. **Temperature:** Warm temperatures not below 60°F (16°C) at night. **Soil:** Use osmunda fiber or fir bark. **Fertilization:** Feed weekly with quarter-strength fertilizer. **Propagation:** Take stem cuttings or separate plantlets. **Special Care:** Needs very high humidity; grow in a greenhouse.

115

## VELTHEIMIA (Forest Lily)

These unusual plants are winter-flowering specimens native to southern Africa. The strap-shaped wavy-edged foliage appears in fall, followed by a tall spike bearing up to fifty tubular flowers. *V. capensis* (top) has dull green leaves and pale pink flowers with green tips. *V. viridifolia* has glossy green leaves and the flowers are pinkish-purple with yellow spots.

**Light:** Four hours of direct sun; shade flowers from noon sun. **Water:** Keep soil moist during growth; allow to dry somewhat while dormant. **Temperature:** Keep newly potted bulbs warm; when shoots emerge, keep about 55°F (13°C). **Soil:** Standard potting mix. **Fertilization:** Feed monthly during growth, beginning after leaves emerge. **Propagation:** Divide bulbs every few years. **Special Care:** When flowering is over, gradually withhold water until foliage dies. Store bulb in pot.

## VRIESEA (Painted-Feather, Flaming-Sword, King-of-Bromeliads)

Many species and hybrids of this large genus of bromeliads are cultivated either for their remarkably colorful banded foliage, or for their vivid flowering stalks. The stalks are long lasting, remaining showy for about six months. Two species are particularly popular because they offer both stunning foliage and flowers. *V. guttata* has inch-wide green leaves mottled with purple or brown and a stalk of shocking pink bracts that display short-lived yellow blossoms. *V. splendens* (middle), flaming-sword, has green leaves with brown crossbands, brilliant red bracts and yellow flowers. 'Rex' (bottom), a hybrid of *V. splendens,* has olive-green foliage and scarlet bracts.

Another very popular species is *V. hieroglyphica,* king-of-bromeliads, which has glossy green leaves with unusual purple markings resembling hieroglyphics. Its flowering stalk is less showy than those of other species, since it is green and bears yellow flowers.

**Light:** Bright indirect light. **Water:** Allow soil to dry somewhat between waterings. Keep vase formed by foliage full of water. **Temperature:** Warm room temperatures above 60°F (16°C) in winter. **Soil:** Use terrestrial bromeliad mix. **Fertilization:** Apply quarter-strength fertilizer to the vase once a month during growth. **Propagation:** Divide offsets after main plant begins to yellow. **Special Care:** Needs high humidity. Mist frequently and grow on a pebble tray. The main plant dies after flowering, but this may take six months to a year. To encourage offsets to flower, place two-year-old plants in a plastic bag with an apple for one week.

116

**WASHINGTONIA filifera** (Desert Fan Palm)
This distinctive palm is rarely grown as a pot plant, but is frequently seen as a street tree in California where its tall trunk is cloaked with a skirt of brown dead foliage. The gray-green fan-shaped leaves are divided into sharp-pointed segments that have many fine curling threads decorating their margins. As a houseplant, this palm requires much more light than most palms.

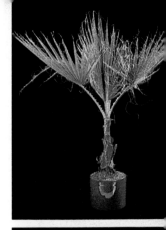

**Light:** Full sun; shade from noon sun in summer. **Water:** Keep moist during growing season and allow to dry somewhat between waterings in winter. **Temperature:** Normal room temperatures; tolerates cold in winter. **Soil:** Standard potting mix with extra loam. **Fertilization:** Feed every two weeks during growth. **Propagation:** Sow fresh seeds. **Special Care:** Needs moderate to high humidity.

**YUCCA** (Yucca, Spanish-Bayonet, Spineless Yucca, Spanish-Dagger)
A tall, sturdy trunk topped with a rosette of stiff, spreading, swordlike foliage gives the yucca a dramatic silhouette that is a perfect accent for a room furnished in modern decor. Several species of these semi-succulent desert plants make good houseplants if they can be given enough sun and cool room temperatures in winter.

Spanish-bayonet (middle), *Y. aloifolia*, has a slender trunk that may be straight or branched, and is topped with very sharp, stiff blue-green leaves. The leaves are so sharp that the plant can pose quite a danger and should be placed in an out-of-the-way location. Several varieties with white- or yellow-striped leaves and with rigid or flexible foliage are popular.

*Y. elephantipes*, the spineless yucca, is a less treacherous plant since the foliage is more flexible and lacks sharp points. The Spanish-dagger (bottom), *Y. gloriosa*, has very stiff leaves with needlelike tips and rough edges. If given plenty of sun, a yucca will usually grow about six feet tall. Large yuccas are especially attractive when several plants of varying heights are arranged in a single large tub.

**Light:** A southern exposure is best; tolerates curtain-filtered sun and bright indirect light. **Water:** Allow soil to dry somewhat between waterings during growth; allow to dry more in winter. **Temperature:** Normal room temperatures during growth; needs about 50°F (10°C) in winter. **Soil:** Standard potting mix. **Fertilization:** Do not fertilize if plant is repotted every year; feed once in spring if not repotting. **Propagation:** Take stem cuttings; trunk will sprout new foliage if cut back to one foot. **Special Care:** Low humidity.

117

**ZANTEDESCHIA** (Calla Lily, Arum Lily)

The elegant blossom of the calla lily consists of a waxy trumpet-shaped bract curling around a spike of tiny flowers and appears above clumps of arrow-shaped leaves. *A. aethiopica* (top) features pure white bracts. *Z. elliottina* has golden bracts and *Z. rehmanii* has pink ones. Calla lilies need a wet growing season and a dry dormant season if they are to thrive and rebloom. **Light:** Full sun; shade from noon sun in summer. **Water:** Keep soil wet during growth, allow to dry somewhat during dormancy. **Temperature:** Normal room temperatures. **Soil:** Standard potting mix. **Fertilization:** Feed weekly during growth with quarter-strength fertilizer. **Propagation:** Divide dormant rhizomes. **Special Care:** After flowering, withhold water and allow plant to go dormant for several months.

**ZEBRINA pendula** (Wandering Jew, Inch Plant)

Species of *Zebrina* and *Tradescantia*, with their colorful pointed leaves that clasp tightly around creeping stems, are so similar in appearance that they have the same common names! *Z. pendula* features white-striped leaves with purple undersides. 'Quadricolor' (middle) has leaves marked on top with silver, green and purple. 'Purpusii' has reddish-green foliage. **Light:** Bright indirect light. **Water:** Allow soil to dry slightly between waterings. **Temperature:** Normal room temperatures down to 50°F (10°C) at night. **Soil:** Standard potting mix. **Fertilization:** Feed monthly while in growth. **Propagation:** Take stem cuttings. **Special Care:** Bare spindly growth is from low light. Limp yellow-spotted leaves are due to overwatering. Cut back old straggly stems.

**ZYGOCACTUS** (Christmas Cactus, Thanksgiving Cactus)

Two jungle cacti, Christmas cactus (bottom), *Z. bridgesii*, and Thanksgiving cactus, *Z. truncata*, are named after the holiday seasons during which they bloom. Christmas cactus has scallop-edged stems and Thanksgiving cactus has jagged edges. Their satiny flowers come in shades of pink, magenta, salmon, or white tinged with violet. These cacti are often listed as *Schlumbergera*. **Light:** Bright indirect light. **Water:** Keep moist during growth; allow to dry somewhat after flowering. **Temperature:** Needs nights of 50° to 55°F (10° to 13°C) in the fall to bloom. **Soil:** Standard potting mix. **Fertilization:** Feed every two weeks during growth with low-nitrogen fertilizer. **Propagation:** Take stem cuttings. **Special Care:** If nights are above 55°F (13°C), plant will need natural day length to flower.

118

# PLANT SELECTION TABLES

These tables will help you choose suitable plants for any location in your home. After you have checked the light and temperature conditions of the area, select a plant from the appropriate chart. Then look up the plant entry to find out if there are any other special requirements. Plants appearing in more than one category will easily adapt to either condition.

## NORTHERN

**Warm Winter**   Above 60°F (16°C)

| | | | |
|---|---|---|---|
| Aglaonema | Caladium | Fittonia | Piper |
| Aspidistra | Didymochlaena | Phlebodium | Saintpaulia |
| Blechnum | | | |

**Cool Winter**   Between 50° to 60°F (10° to 16°C)

| | | | |
|---|---|---|---|
| Aspidistra | Dracaena | Phyllitis | Saxifraga |
| Asplenium | Gasteria | Primula | Soleirolia |
| Begonia | Microlepia | Rechsteineria | Tetrastigma |
| Cyclamen | Nephrolepis | Sansevieria | |

**Cold Winter**   Below 50°F (10°C)

Ampelopsis brevipedunculata

## LOW LIGHT/INTERIOR LIGHT

**Warm Winter**   Above 60°F (16°C)

| | | | |
|---|---|---|---|
| Aglaonema | Dieffenbachia | Pseuderanthemum | Spathiphyllum |
| Aspidistra | Dipteracanthus | (curtain-filtered) | Syngonium |
| Cyperus | Peperomia | Rhaphidophora | (green varieties) |

**Cool Winter**   Between 50° to 60°F (10° to 16°C)

| | | | |
|---|---|---|---|
| Acorus | Cyrtomium | Hedera | Philodendron |
| (green varieties) | Dracaena | Howea | Phyllitis |
| Asparagus | Fatshedera | Hoya | Sansevieria |
| Aspidistra | Fatsia | Microlepia | Schefflera |
| Cissus | Ficus | Monstera | Tolmiea |

**Cold Winter**   Below 50°F (10°C)

Ophiopogon

# 4 HOURS OF DIRECT SUN

**Warm Winter**  Above 60°F (16°C)

Acalypha
Allamanda
Billbergia
Capsicum
Codiaeum
 (eastern)
Coleus
 (eastern)
Cordyline
Cyperus
Euphorbia
Gardenia
 (eastern)

Guzmania
Gynura
 (eastern)
Hippeastrum
Hymenocallis
Impatiens
 (curtain-filtered)
Ipomoea
Iresine
Jacaranda
Jacobinia
Olea
Oreopanax

Peperomia
 (curtain-filtered)
Phlebodium
 (curtain-filtered)
Pisonia
Polyscias
 (curtain-filtered)
Rhaphidophora
 (curtain-filtered)
Saintpaulia
 (curtain-filtered)
Sinningia
 (curtain-filtered)

Smithiantha
 (curtain-filtered;
 eastern)
Sprekelia
Streptocarpus
 (eastern)

**Cool Winter**  Between 50° to 60°F (10° to 16°C)

Abutilon
Aporocactus
Asparagus
Beloperone
Ceropegia
Chamaerops
Cissus
Cotyledon
Crassula
Cuphea
Cymbidium
Cyrtomium
Echeveria
Espostoa
Eugenia
Ficus
 (eastern)
Fuchsia
 (eastern;
 no noon sun)

Gasteria
Gloriosa
Grevillea
 (no noon sun)
Gymnocalycium
Haemanthus
Haworthia
 (curtain-filtered)
Hedera
Hibiscus
Hoya
Hydrangea
 (eastern)
Lampranthus
Lithops
Lycaste
 (eastern)
Mikania
Musa

Nephrolepsis
 (curtain-filtered;
 eastern)
Nertera
 (eastern)
Notocactus
Odontoglossum
 (eastern)
Oplismenus
Oxalis
Pacypodium
Parodia
Passiflora
Pellaea
Phoenix
Platycerium
 (curtain-filtered)
Plectranthus
 (eastern)

Pteris
 (curtain-filtered;
 eastern)
Senecio
Setcreasea
Solanum
 (eastern)
Thunbergia
Vallota
Veltheimia
Washingtonia
Yucca
Zantedeschia

| Cold Winter | Below 50°F (10°C) | | |
| --- | --- | --- | --- |
| Aeonium | Echinopsis | Lobivia | Sedum |
| Agave | Epidendrum | Mammillaria | Skimmia |
| Aporocactus | (cane-forming | (no noon sun) | (eastern) |
| Astrophytum | kinds; eastern) | Opuntia | Stapelia |
| Cephalocereus | Faucaria | Pittosporum | |
| Cereus | Hebe | Podocarpus | |
| Conophytum | Jasminum | (curtain-filtered) | |
| (eastern) | (no noon sun) | Rebutia | |
| Duchesnea | Laurus | Rhododendron | |
| (no noon sun) | (eastern) | (eastern) | |

# BRIGHT INDIRECT LIGHT

**Warm Winter**   Above 60°F (16°C)

| Acalypha | Chlorophytum | Impatiens | Rhaphidophora |
| --- | --- | --- | --- |
| Achimenes | Cissus | Kohleria | (curtain-filtered) |
| Aechmea | Codiaeum | Maranta | Scindapsus |
| Aeschynanthus | Codonanthe | Medinilla | Siderasis |
| Alocasia | Cordyline | Nepenthes | Sonerila |
| Anthurium | Cyperus | Pandanus | Spathiphyllum |
| Aphelandra | Didymochlaena | Paphiopedilum | Stenandrium |
| Billbergia | Dieffenbachia | (mottled-leaved) | Stromanthe |
| Blechnum | Dipteracanthus | Peperomia | Syngonium |
| Browallia | Dizygotheca | Perilepta | (variegated) |
| Caladium | Episcia | Pilea | Tillandsia |
| Calathea | Fittonia | Piper | Vriesea |
| Callisia | Hypoestes | Pseuderanthemum | |

**Cool Winter**   Between 50° to 60°F (10° to 16°C)

| Acorus | Begonia | Chrysanthemum | Cyclamen |
| --- | --- | --- | --- |
| (variegated) | Brunfelsia | Cissus | Cyrtomium |
| Adiantum | Calanthe | Clerodendrum | Dipladenia |
| Aporocactus | Calceolaria | Cleyera | Dracaena |
| Araucaria | Campanula | Clivia | Epiphyllum |
| Ardisia | Chamaedorea | Coffea | Exacum |
| Asparagus | Chamaerops | Columnea | Fatshedera |
| Asplenium | Chlorophytum | Crossandra | Fatsia |

*(Continued)*

| | | | |
|---|---|---|---|
| Ficus | Nephrolepis | Pilea | Scirpus |
| Gasteria | Nertera | Platycerium | Senecio |
| Gloriosa | Oplismenus | Plectranthus | Setcreasea |
| Guzmania | Pachystachys | Primula | Soleirolia |
| Hedera | Paphiopedilum | Pteris | Sparmannia |
| Howea | (green-leaved) | Rechsteineria | Tetrastigma |
| Hoya | Pedilanthus | Rhipsalidopsis | Tolmiea |
| Microcoelum | Pellaea | Rhoeo | Tradescantia |
| Microlepia | Peperomia | Sansevieria | Yucca |
| Monstera | Pellionia | Saxifraga | Zebrina |
| Narcissus | Philodendron | Schefflera | Zygocactus |
| Neoregelia | Phoenix | | |

**Cold Winter** Below 50°F (10°C)

| | | | |
|---|---|---|---|
| Aeonium | Conophytum | Duchesnea | Ophiopogon |
| Ampelopsis | Cytisus | Erica | Rhoicissus |
| Astrophytum | Datura | Liriope | Senecio |

# SOUTHERN
## (ALL-DAY SUN)
**Warm Winter** Above 60°F (16°C)

| | | | |
|---|---|---|---|
| Aeschynanthus | Dizygotheca | Ipomoea | Pelargonium |
| Alocasia | (curtain-filtered) | Iresine | Pisonia |
| Ananas | Episcia | Jacobinia | Tillandsia |
| Browallia | (curtain-filtered) | (curtain-filtered) | (curtain-filtered) |
| Calanthe | Hypoestes | Kohleria | Torenia |
| (curtain-filtered) | (curtain-filtered) | (curtain-filtered) | (curtain-filtered) |
| Callisia | Impatiens | Musa | Vanda |
| (curtain-filtered) | (curtain-filtered) | (curtain-filtered) | |
| Catharanthus | | | |
| (curtain-filtered) | | | |

**Cool Winter**   Between 50° to 60°F (10° to 16°C)

| | | | |
|---|---|---|---|
| Aloe | Hoya | Mikania | Schefflera |
| Bougainvillea | Hyacinthus | (curtain-filtered) | Stephanotis |
| Campanula | (curtain-filtered) | Narcissus | (curtain-filtered) |
| (curtain-filtered) | Hypocyrta | (curtain-filtered) | Tolmiea |
| Citrofortunella | (curtain-filtered) | Neoregelia | (curtain-filtered) |
| Crassula | Jacobinia | (curtain-filtered) | Tradescantia |
| (curtain-filtered) | (curtain-filtered) | Passiflora | (curtain-filtered) |
| Dipladenia | Kalanchoe | Pedilanthus | Tulipa |
| (curtain-filtered) | Lycaste | (curtain-filtered) | Washingtonia |
| Exacum | (curtain-filtered) | Persea | Yucca |
| (curtain-filtered) | Microcoelum | (curtain-filtered) | Zantedeschia |
| Haworthia | (curtain-filtered) | Plectranthus | |
| (curtain-filtered) | Microlepia | (curtain-filtered) | |
| Howea | (curtain-filtered) | Plumbago | |
| (curtain-filtered) | | | |

**Cold Winter**   Below 50°F (10°C)

| | | | |
|---|---|---|---|
| Acacia | Epidendrum | Laurus | Nerium |
| Agapanthus | (no noon sun) | (curtain-filtered) | Pelargonium |
| Callistemon | Erica | Liriope | Pittosporum |
| Cytisus | (curtain-filtered) | (curtain-filtered) | Stenocarpus |
| Datura | Ferocactus | Neoporteria | (curtain-filtered) |
| Echinocactus | Hydrangea | (curtain-filtered) | |

## EASY-TO-GROW PLANTS

| | | | |
|---|---|---|---|
| Asparagus densiflorus | Coleus | Philodendron scandens | Tradescantia |
| Aspidistra | Crassula argentea | Rhaphidophora | Zebrina |
| Chamaedorea | Ficus elastica | Sansevieria | |
| Cissus rhombifolia | Hoya carnosa | Syngonium | |

# INDEX